22/10
80p

THIS BOOK
BELONGS TO:
Catherine
Milnes

CLASSIFICATION: POETRY

A CIP catalogue record for this book is available from
the British Library.

Printed and bound in Great Britain.

This Midlands, East Anglia and South West
edition

ISBN 1-84436-015-6

First published in Great Britain in 2003 by
United Press Ltd
Admail 3735
London
EC1B 1JB
Tel: 0870 240 6190
Fax: 0870 240 6191
ISBN for complete set of volumes
1-84436-013-X
All Rights Reserved

www.unitedpress.co.uk

Dazzled
by the
Moon

4

Foreword

The title of this book was inspired by a very poetic quotation. As soon as I saw that quotation, I was struck by its poignancy.

I'm an avid writer of poetry myself, and when I gaze at the beauty of a bright moon on a cool, clear night, I'm always struck by its magnificence and majesty. Sometimes I'm even inspired to wax poetic, and I'm sure the moon has, throughout the ages, had the same effect on millions of people.

Throughout the history of man, the moon has been the inspiration for poets, musicians and artists in all forms of creativity.

And the poets brought together in this collection all display that same gift for expressiveness. Their work is put together in this collection for your entertainment and edification. We sincerely hope that you find something from these pages to *dazzle* your imagination.

Peter Quinn, Editor.

Contents

The poets who have contributed to this volume are listed below, along with the relevant page upon which their work can be found.

62	Christopher M Harris	89	David Wareham
63	Charlotte Thompson		Jacqui Hancox
	Arthur Barlow	90	Richard Rochester
64	Alistair J R Ball	91	Mary Ricketts
	Sylvie Wright	92	Graham Smith
65	Kelvin Donaghey	93	M S Reid
	Dylan Pugh		Frances Bowman
66	Julie Hill	94	Kirsty Timmins
67	Jenny Lynch		Hilary Cairns
	Roy Iliffe	95	Phillipa George
68	Lee Busby	96	Sandra Benson
	Michelle Ritchie		Derek Hughes
69	Emma Stannard	97	John Hopkins
	Jessica Furse	98	Doreen Roys
70	Ben Scanlan	99	Elizabeth Morris
	Alex McQuade		Tasmin Hembery
71	Sophie Nuttall	100	George Shipley
	F J Dunn	101	Ann Carratt
72	Robin Morgan	102	Mark Orchard
	Iris Covell	103	Hilary Malone
73	Michael Doughty	104	Nadia Martelli
	Margaret Todd		V A Shardlow
74	Jane Glover	105	Eilise Lindop
	Elizabeth Chivers	106	Edmund Hunt
75	Donald Turner	107	Edna J Insley
	Heidi Charlton	107	Carol Underwood
76	Paddy O'Neill	108	Beryl Johnson
	Joan Daines	109	Rebecca Bromham
77	Mitch Cokien	110	Alistair Morgan
78	Philip Johnson		Timothy Jones
79	Paul Hughes	111	George Payne
80	Patrick Smith	112	Linda Cleveland
81	Hayley Nixon	113	Rex Collinson
82	Norman Meadows	114	Farrah Sassani
83	John Russell Telford		Maria Benedicta Ward
84	Keith L Powell	115	Ian Finch
85	Daniel Stannard	116	Lee Mummery
86	John Davies	117	Paul Fisk
	Diana Cockrill	118	Jackie Johnson
87	Margaret Whitworth	119	Dennis Theobald
	William Milligan	120	Sarah Eden
88	Steve Blyth		Sarah Elsdon
	John Howlett	121	Joyce Barton

	Belinda Budgen		Sally Boyd'Robinson
122	Gina Arnold	150	Clive Blake
	Bryony	151	Peter Petrauske
123	Yvonne Allen	152	J A Murtagh
	Sean O'Brien		Penny Kirby
124	Diane Stevens	153	Pauline Bulmer
125	Mark Andrews		Marcella Pellow
126	Peter Day	154	Penelope Hornsey
	Natalie Knowles	155	Jacqueline Urch
127	Georgina Treeves		Val Davis
128	Ray Coleman	156	Margaret Cobbledick
129	Sarah Godbeer		Cassandra May
	Sarah Bidgood		Poultney
130	Hazel Williams	157	Margaret Beaumont
131	Betty Harcombe	158	Lucy Wilson
132	Valerie Ann	159	Valentine Hammett
	Shearstone		Rebecca Kindred
	Eileen Fitton	160	E Gwen Gardner
133	Eleanor MacNair	161	Richie Eves
	Jonathan Lawson	162	Claire Shepherd
134	Stuart Barrass		Christine Smith
135	John R Tattersall	163	Rona Laycock
	Joan Kernick	164	Claire Wright
136	Sarah Jones	165	Bob Wilson
137	Miriam Penna	166	Brian D Lancaster
138	Christine Hall	167	Barney Sprague
	Anna Gorjatseva		Angharad Williams
139	Grace Edna Tomes	168	Jimima Shaw
	Audrey Ingram		Peter Gillott
140	Michael Davis	169	Lorna Harding
	Ted Harriott	170	Paul M Thomas
141	Phyllis Henderson	171	Natasha Stoakes
	Martin Ellis		Philippa Adburgham
142	Ruth Rowland	172	Elana Freeman
143	Janine Vallor	173	Joan Lake
144	Sylvia Wilson	174	Ann Beard
145	Tereza Rule	175	Laura Butcher
146	Pete Basten	176	Dave Stockley
	Jonathan Taylor	177	Jane Marshall
147	Gail Whitson	178	Matt Bartlett
	Heather D Woon	179	John Morgan
148	Cheryl Morrison	180	Gerald Whyte
149	Charlotte Rice	181	Carolyn Fittall

9

PERFECT

A perfect journey through this perfect vale,
Filled with the scents and colours of spring.
Pastel blossoms filling the air with fragrance.
White clouds floating in a soft, blue sky, filled
With promises. New season, new hopes, new beginnings.

A rare delight for my precious, perfect mother, but,
Eyes, tear-filled, spoke volumes. She smiled, bravely.
I saw her then, so small, so fragile, so vulnerable,
And suddenly, so very old. My heart was heavy.
On that day that was so perfect, I knew the truth.
I held her, and together, we kept our silence.

Here in the ambulance, in my heart, I said "Goodbye."
And here, I silently said "Forgive me."
Soon, she would begin her final journey.
My prayers were for another perfect day.
And perfect peace.
And, here, in the ambulance, I silently said "Goodbye."
She smiled. She squeezed my hand.
And I knew she understood.

Audrey Brown, Worcester, Worcestershire

Born in Lancashire **Audrey Brown** has interests including
music, art and needlecraft. "I have always been interested in
poems and my work is influenced by Alzheimer's Disease,"
she said. "It led me to serious thought. Until then I was a
happy-go-lucky and self-centred person. My style is honest
and down-to-earth. My work is written with a great deal of
thought and reflection on my life. I would like to be remem-
bered as a person who always tried her best at everything."
Aged 75, she has had several careers and has an ambition to
continue enjoying life. She is a widow with two children and
two grandchildren. "The person I would most like to meet is
the Queen," she added. "I wouldn't change places with her at
any price but admire her tremendously."

LONGING FOR A LOVE LOST

Can we recall those halcyon days?
And love's sweet nostalgic summer haze.
The rashness of forgotten youth,
When all we searched for was the truth.
Has the wisdom of our autumn years,
Dried those adolescent tears?
If we had the fortune to return,
To a love-laced spring, would we spurn
A heartbeat's call to lover's arms
An arrow fired with Cupid's charms.
With the bitter-sweet romantic pain,
And a desire that flowed like falling rain?

Kenneth Powell, St Johns, Worcester, Worcestershire

MUM

She says black
I say white
She says no
I say yes
You can't wear that
Yes I can
He's no good
I love him
When she spoke
I should have listened
She was right
I was wrong
Now I'm a mother
The lessons have been learnt
I say black
And she agrees

Margaret Darrington, Ross-on-Wye, Herefordshire

MATTHEW, ONE WEEK OLD

Gently, I rock you
Gazing at each other
For the first time.

Your eyes so blue
Looking round intently,
Learning about the world.

You nestle against me
Soft as thistledown,
Relaxed and happy.

You nuzzle my dress
Our first grandchild.
Deep contentment.

No frowns today
Your mum is here
And dinner's ready.

Jane Cox, Leominster, Herefordshire

LUCY

She has a golden quilt,
the child who cannot play,
it shimmers like the sunshine
on a bright summer's day.

Small hands gently resting,
pale fingers softly furled,
lovely brown eyes gazing
on a curious crowded world.

On all those busy grown-ups,
who find the time to spare,
to stroke her arm and say kind
words, to show they really care.

Dark hair flows on her pillow,
while her mother's tender touch,
brings cheer and consolation
to a girl who needs so much.

Though she'll never run or skip,
or dance the night away,
she's wrapped up in a quilt of love,
the child who cannot play.

Sonja F Mills, Redditch, Worcestershire

MY GRANDDAUGHTER ISIS

The black thorn petals fall
as soft and white as snow
The swing sways gently
waiting for the child who will not come
The loudest of groaning
passes through the *straif*
Coercion comes from out and in
The world forces and controls
Those who must make the choice
if the child will come one day
To play upon my swing
Be patient.
Wait and see
I'll make a black rod wand
and turn its magic, petal white
To change coercion into right

Margot Miller, Fownhope, Herefordshire

Margot Miller said: "*Straif* is the old Irish word for black-thorn - one of the 25 trees of the Celtic ogham alphabet - meaning coercion, and a period of waiting patiently. This is part of a long poem begun in 1995, a further verse added each year in the life of my granddaughter Isis, queen of the heavens, and Makeda, queen of Sheba. Of course, this poem is dedicated to Isis and Makeda, and their new brother born in May 2003. I have written an historical novel *The Priestess of Ennor, a Celtic Journey* and a book on the Celtic ogham tree alphabet; at present I am working on *The Zodiac In The Wye Valley Landscape.*"

I'LL WAIT ON THE SHELF

If I should die for goodness sake
An urn on the mantle I will make
Keep me there till you can join me
Then we will follow a path to the sea.

Our ashes joined in a flowing bond
Into the Salwerpe, then beyond
To the Severn, and then to the sea
An eternal bond for you and me.

We will visit the places, never been
See the coastlines we never have seen
Hand in hand our spirits will wander
Our love forever, no more asunder.

An invisible heaven under the sea
A timeless life for you and me
All in the future not yet I hope
A lot more years before the slope.

Ivor Wakelam, Droitwich Spa, Worcestershire

ANGUISH

Loneliness
The feeling of failure is all-consuming.
As your feet; your shoes like lead weights
Move like concrete blocks across the floor.
Attention on you for all the wrong reasons
You did not strive all your life for this humiliation.

You prepare for relative obscurity
Your rise so meteoric, and your fall so damning.
But while a weaker man would have been
Instantaneously crushed to a pulp.
You held on, and with characteristic grit, refused to yield.

Constant scrutiny tracks your flight.
The drawbridge of your castle is now, finally, raised.
Stay there, safe, my sweet.
I will hold you close.
Protecting you,
But only in my dreams.

Kirsty Wilkes, Kidderminster, Worcestershire

MISTS AND SHADOWS

Deep within the shadows of my mind,
Obscured by mists of passing time,
A memory stirs.
And, as the years begin to fall away,
Once more I am with you, on that summer's day.
Heather-covered mountains rise towards the skies,
Their majesty and splendour reflected in your eyes.
I see the sparkling waters of a loch
Where you gave me flowers,
Not the sort that sit on market stalls for hours,
But a sweet bouquet of wild, windswept blooms
With hedgerow names, and fresh perfume.
Ours was but a short encounter,
Out paths crossed once, through time,
And when we said goodbye, my love I left behind.
The mists and shadows once more descend,
They hide you once again,
But, in my heart, locked away,
The memory will remain.

Carol Hooper, Lower Broadheath, Worcestershire

THE LAST PHOTOGRAPH

To stand here and think of you
Fills my heart with a burgeoning pride
Your ways so pure, deeds so kindly
Your snowflake hair and bluebell eyes
Worried hands fidgeting, blue veins bursting

I feel your pride
I see the merry twinkle in your eyes
Memories so precious even then
And so dear now to me

I smell your brow, your innocence returned
You smelt like a flower
I draw the sweet, wondrous smell of you down deep
Never to be forgotten

Your music plays within my heart
I hear it always
You made a part of me
That will always be there.

Patricia Clark, Evesham, Worcestershire

UNCOVER

Silently, violently, openly, gone,
The dreamer was shattered by what went on.
In a haze of bewilderment,
In a blur of deceit,
The truth was uncovered,
And fell to my feet.
It's a curious thing that dreams can disguise,
Something quite different, the worst surprise.

Susie Belt, Worcester, Worcestershire

BEHIND THE SMILE

It's raining in my heart
I'm smiling, yes, I know
But I learnt to conceal, not to reveal,
My pain and vulnerability,
Oh yes, and my sheer stupidity
At allowing myself a little taste of what could be,
But never will.
Knowing as I do that I can never have you,
For more than a moment or two,
In this vast expanse of time.
Precious moments when you will only see,
The smiles of love and happiness that you bring to me.
And if behind your smile,
It's raining in your heart.
Remember how the sun shines when we are not apart.
Look forward to the days,
When storm clouds roll away,
Bringing us together, on yet another, sunny day.

Carol Graham, Hereford, Herefordshire

FANCY PACKAGING

I hate the way you look
As you glide around the place
With your make-up like a film star
And your hair an aura round your face

I hate the way your hair flows
Like golden strands, mine's greasy with no shine
Your clothes make you look slender
While my fat spills out of mine

I hate your skin so perfect
It's silky and icy pale
While I pluck my moustache daily
To stop me looking like a male

I hate the way you eat
You gorge and still stay thin
I only have to see a chip
And out pops another chin

I might hate the way you look
But you have a heart of stone
I have loving friends and family
So will never be alone

Anita Longmuir, Droitwich Spa, Worcestershire

ASSESSMENT

Through rain-grained windows,
To the road-waved hill,
The struggling wind,
Billows my mind,
Readily to the past,
With thoughts smoothed by time,
And happenings perfect.
Of memories sprayed by tears
and sadness,
Of follies, weaknesses and regrets,
Not lasting, diminished the more,
With the happiness of living and
The beauty of loving.

Idwal T Davies, Kidderminster, Worcestershire

WOMBSTONE

When I hold a piece of rock
In my palm
It is you I hold in my heart.
"Feel the power in this"
You'd say of one,
Quarrying another
Handful of pebbles from a small pocket.
How fitting that you, after all these years,
Too early emerged from your cave,
A precious gemstone
Named and prepared,
In case your premature formation
Should prove to be fool's gold,
Could be still, so ever in love, with the earth's cobbles.

Cheryl V Nethersole, Holme Lacy, Herefordshire

SOUTHERN MEMORY

The person I kissed in the porch
Wasn't you,
On those vibrant evenings
When darkness was broken
By sparkling lights
In the unknown neighbourhood,
And crickets chanted
Through the subdued throb
Of music in unknown houses.

It should have been you I kissed
In the porch,
But it was someone else;
You and I sat stiffly, side by side
On the sofa in the parlour,
Inches apart, exchanging views,
And when it was time for you to go
Nothing happened, not even
The last time.

Dorothy Buyers, Oswestry, Shropshire

HE

He, reflection of my senility,
He, mirror of my age, bent and broken
Leads me to my measurement bespoken,
Batten'd away for all eternity.
He, whose barren day is but sympathy,
He, whose night is just some mere token;
Night and day to him remain unwoken,
Awake in me, an imaged parody.
The years heap'd forward, what do they bestow:
The quest of youth? The everlasting hill
That blights our progress? Now it's winter's cold,
Walk we all each with lengthening shadow
The morning rays have faded; we are old
Our faltering steps retard, and then are still.

Bernard W Grace, Whitchurch, Shropshire

JRB

Jasmine sweet, I breathe in deep
a forest I breathe out
fire glow for all who know
my beautiful tree without doubt.

Reach up high with no goodbye
entwined with balmy dew
your spirit raise with tender praise
the world's my gift for you.

Bright flowers with every hour
a florid gift of pleasure
enchanted soul, my levitated goal
my tree, my child, my treasure.

Donna-Marie Robertson, Whittington, Shropshire

I FELL IN LOVE WITH THE GYPSY

The smell of woodsmoke filled the air,
As fiddlers played and spoons tapped on a knee.
The ladies danced and swirled their skirts
All around the campfire, wild and free.

The music grew faster, the dancing more wild,
And Darky the Gypsy, stood beside a tree.
With raven black curls and large black eyes,
He glanced across, smiled and that moment belonged to
me.

Twigs crackled and bright flame danced upon the fire.
Men sang songs of old, children clapped with glee.
Soon it all became a blur, heart pounding, pulse racing
He was walking right over to me.

Time slowed, as I drifted into heaven on earth.
He took me in his arms and we danced together as one.
Then I knew where I wanted to be for years to come
So I joined my Romany Gypsy, my old life now gone.

Ann Chadwick, Bridgnorth, Shropshire

LETTING DOWN THE SUMMER DRESSES

Sitting on a park bench,
letting down the hems
of my daughter's summer dresses,
the stranger by my side touched the
floral printed cotton and
lined flecked with daisies.

Her restless fingers lingered
over last year's captive creases,
tracing faded maps of fruit stains
from the season's crop of berries.
Then the smile that slowly ruptured,
dismembering her features,
broke like the sun withdrawing,
and her tears distilled mascara,
splashing wetly on the daisies.

"I haven't cried till now, you know
I couldn't cry.
My daughter died a week ago
and summer memories haunt me so,"
She said, "So young to die."

Margaret Whitaker, Shrewsbury, Shropshire

ELLIE

Sweet baby body
Pressed naked, close to mine
Baby breath
Child of child of mine.
Gentle fingers grasping,
Touching
Big green eyes
Directly watching
Seeing far beyond
These eyes of ours.
Now sleeping
Quite abandoned
Trusting, innocent
Hair spread around
The pillow
Red in tint
And baby fine
Melts my heart
Blessed baby
Child of child of mine.

Janice Higgins, Bishops Castle, Shropshire

OUR LOVE IS

Deep as the dark
Hollowed out holes
In the damp sand

Shining as the light
Reflecting off pebbles
Wet from the sea

Laughing as the carefree
Child playing games
As waves lap the shore

Warm as the sun
Shimmering across
The evening sky

Smiling as the moonbeams
Shine across sandcastles
Taken by the tide

True as the ocean
Is eternally
Brought to the shore

Julie Copeland, Fenton, Staffordshire

GROWING PAINS

With pride I've watched my grandson
grow to over six foot tall
I'd dreamed he'd take up medicine
or hear some noble call.

I know he has a safe retreat
to share with teenage friends,
loud music and funny jokes
an exchange of modern trends.

One day I was more than curious
refreshments I took to share
But oh, his new found love stood
stripped right down and bare.

It's not for me to judge if
talent lies in his hands,
a pre-conceived genetic force
has scuppered well laid plans.

I'm trusting he will ponder as
he renews his piston rings
and know his bike was but an object
in a quest of greater things.

Olive Bedford, Tutbury, Burton-on-Trent, Staffordshire

A VISIT TO BERRINGTON HALL

Portraits of our ancestors hang upon the walls,
In silence, not seeing nor hearing
But only facing us.
We walk along the corridors through the many rooms,
Seeing all those who had lived here
Just looking down on us.

The children's room holds many favourite toys and games,
Now there is no screaming, no speaking
While children smile at us.
The scratches and the fingerprints do not go with time,
Nor do little children ever move
They only stare at us.

In the courtyard and the garden, statues always stand,
Weather-beaten but never moaning
Just greeting all of us.
Time rolls ever onward and visitors all must age
But lone portraits and stone effigies
Change not in front of us.

Jenkyn Evans, Wombourne, Staffordshire

IMMORTAL

I found you in a book
I saw you from light
That shone back into the room.
Philosophers and kings
Vagabonds and priests
All at once held you in awe.
Centuries pass, but you remain.
I spied you from afar
Saw you naked in darkness
That enshrouded in the night.
Poets and artists
Lovers and teachers
Dare not speak your name.
Whichever way I turn
I shall be with you.
In a book I saw you
Moonlight ran through you
As you gazed into my room
And then I walked to the horizon
And you welcomed me.

Andrew Handsaker, Burton-on-Trent, Staffordshire

TO MY KINDLY GARDENER

I feel inclined to write some
Little witty lines to you
You are so very kind to me
I cannot understand it,
What have I done to cause you, sir,
To be so open-handed.

Your veg are so delicious
And you're delicious too
And though they'll fill me many a plate,
Of which I do appreciate,
I'd much prefer 'twas you.

Joyce Thorley, Moorlands, Staffordshire

HOME

Grandad don't you miss your home?
I know you came here to give us a better life
But grandad don't you miss your home?
The silver beaches, the palm trees
The jungle paths you used to roam
Now you live in a concrete block
Grandad don't you miss your home?
Let me tell you something son
When I go for my morning walk
I walk in silence, never talk
I see my tiger on the leaves of a tree
I see my monkey in a tone on the bridge
The pavement becomes my coral reef
The houses a mountain range, so
You see son, I never really left my
Home, part of it will always be with me
The sea the sand and the palm tree

Stephen Fox, Burton-on-Trent, Staffordshire

THOSE CAREFREE DAYS

What happened to the young lads who whistled away
As they cycled miles to work each day?
And the girls who blushed a pretty shade
When wolf whistled as their journeys they made?

I remember the lamplighter on his bike
How at dusk he arrived to switch on the lights,
In autumn the Scottish fisher girls we watched
As they sorted the herrings when they arrived in the
smacks.

Entertainment was simple, no television then
Church on Sundays, then picking wild flowers in the glen.

Those fresh faced lads to war were sent
To fight for their country, that's where they went,
Those who died were buried where they fell
And those who returned had sad stories to tell.

Those carefree days had gone forever
When as children we played in fields of clover.
Times have changed, nothing ever stays the same
Those carefree days will never return again.

Mollie Carter, Burton-on-Trent, Staffordshire

MEMORIES

Memories O those memories dear
Of happy childhood days
Deserve a special prayer to God
In words of thankful praise
Of music I would never tire
With joyous singing in the choir
Carols with their well-loved tunes
An Eastern Inn with crowded rooms
The new-borne babe in manger bare
With silent ox and ass to stare
A silent night, a holy night
With guiding star that shone so bright
Such memories my heart to cheer
At Christmas time, come once a year
Our family round the humble hearth
To celebrate the Saviour's birth
Lots of presents so much fun
And grateful hearts when all is done

Peter Hugh Bennett, Stratford-upon-Avon, Warwickshire

WHISPERS

The last time I saw you I wore my watch,
Which has since been lost:
Lost - then stolen.

Now and then I think of the two of you
Clasped to someone else's arm,
As once you both clasped mine;
And only now do I hear the whispers of alarm:
"Tick-tock, tick-tock, we haven't got much time."

Simon Gunter, Rugby, Warwickshire

THE PHOTOGRAPH

The photograph hung motionless upon the wall
But the face inside the frame
Was not static at all.
It spoke of action and pain
All in the same restricted space.
The eyes were darkened by experience,
The lashes holding in the emotion
As a fence around
The soul full of devotion
For those he had lost
In the mud and blood
Of Flanders' meadows.
Where a ghostly wind blows
Across the yellowed edges of his tombed frame
His ancient breath give thanks to God
That all gathered now
In those long forgotten fields
Are golden harvest yields.

Pat Bidmead, Nuneaton, Warwickshire

ABSENT

In warm September your spirit I find,
Autumn mists meander in my mind
Through the forest, pierce the sun's rays
Recalling warm lips in passionate display
Branches lift and sway, for nature they hold
Arms that tease and embrace the cold.
Gentle breezes blow silently across the land
Whispering tokens, covered by a lover's hand.
Above a bird shrills loud with song
Oh, love, let us not part for too long.

Victoria Brown, Nuneaton, Warwickshire

IMAGES V

Puppy-lover pushed to putrid ends
Amid confusion of a brittle world.
And being lost, returning home again
To yearn anew for sudden flings.
Spared elemental egress from this world
Reliving torments that such conscience brings.

Thus limbo-like in fantasy, but yet compelled
To blend a pattern from the earthly sphere;
Protesting still with youth's shrill call
Against the torture of unearthly fear.

Till fatally flung diaphanous heartbeat
To dwell with deva-spirits in the light:
And so, angelic daughter of my soul, find peace:
A peace that will consume you till we meet.

Victor Church, Stratford-upon-Avon, Warwickshire

36

MY ANGEL

Bright blue eyes
And a perfect smile
Yes, I love him
No denial

He's beautiful
He's so complete
So many strengths
You can't compete

He is my son
My only one
He's nearly three
Where has time gone?

He is my angel
My bundle of joy
I love him so much
My little boy

Becky Lucas, Bedworth, Warwickshire

OUT OF THE DARKNESS

If I've been waiting;
Anticipating,
Just to feel your sweet caress;
I've come out of the darkness.

Now as I offer my heart to you;
There's no way I want to be apart from you,
As I offer you nothing less;
I've come out of the darkness.

If there's no way of knowing;
It's you love who's got me going,
Now with these words I confess;
I've come out of the darkness.

Now as these words come full circle;
As I'm just waiting for a miracle,
As I feel a little sadness -
For the one I've lost;
As I've just come out of the darkness.

Jeff Warne, Rugby, Warwickshire

MORE THAN A BROTHER

More than a brother,
More than a friend.
I thought our time
Would never end.
Then tragedy struck,
And fate played a part,
But you cheated death -
You live in my heart.

Adam Lowe, Loughborough, Leicestershire

*Words alone could never do you justice. We were proud to
know you and we all miss you still, Joe.*

THE IMPOSSIBLE

The perfect man would need to be;

Generous, but solvent.
Happy, but aware of problems.
Funny, but tasteful.
Passionate, but patient and loving.
Helpful, but unpatronising.
Knowledgeable, but at no time arrogant.
Where can we find this perfect man?

The perfect woman would need to be;

Connoisseur, but food prepared instantly.
Houseproud, but always welcoming.
Caring, but no fussing.
Hardworking, but uncomplaining.
Prudent, but noble.
Career-minded, but always available.
Why are we unable to locate this perfect woman?

Lynda Warren, Rugby, Warwickshire

ABSENT FRIENDS

In the quiet of the evening,
As the shades of night descend,
Sometimes I shed a tear,
When I think of absent friends.

They played a big part,
Within my life,
Much happiness they brought,
My friends to me are priceless,
For friendship can't be bought.

Though many miles divide us,
As we are far apart,
The memories that I have of them,
Are locked within my heart.

So when the day is over,
And their mind from care is free,
When of others they are thinking,
I hope they sometimes think of me.

Margaret Burnip, Nuneaton, Warwickshire

ARTHUR

A scarlet flame
A lion's mane
A mighty roar that split the night.

A cry of woe
A gale that blows
A wreathing fog to blind the sight.

A gleaming sword
A magic word
A warrior king to win the fight.

A lover's part
A broken heart
Abandoned for a country's plight.

A holy quest
A final test
A battle fought 'tween dark and light.

Emma Melville, Nuneaton, Warwickshire

CHILDLESS MOTHER

I will never be able to watch you take your first tentative
steps,
Or hear the first of your long awaiting words.
I will never be able to share with you the magic of bedtime
stories,
Or comfort you from your nightmares.
I will never be able to see you ride your first bike,
Or ease the pain of cuts and grazes if you should fall.
I will never be able to enjoy you playing in the golden sum-
mer sun,
Or nurse you back to health when you are sick.
I will never be able to witness you leaving for your first
date,
Or pick up the pieces of a broken heart.
I will never be able to listen to your hopes and dreams,
Or wipe away your flow of tears and ease your fears.
I will never be able to show you just how much I care,
Or tell you I love you with all of my heart.

Priscilla Clayton, Birmingham, West Midlands

THE COAT

I dreamed of the coat that was so familiar
the texture was rough but the feeling so warm.

Given away at the point of death
And lost forever I thought.

In my dreams I searched, to no avail.
I only wanted to take hold of the warmth that had gone.

But then - years later I found that someone
had snatched up the coat from death's door.
To put in a safe and secure place forevermore.

What elation - disbelief - the tears just flowed
that indeed dreams can come true.

The coat not lost forever - but safe and secure.

Pam Bridgwater, Birmingham, West Midlands

THE GLADIATOR

The smell of fear is all around
Blood and entrails smear the ground
Through the madness hear the sound
Of cheering.

Beads of sweat form on the face
Thumping heart begins to race
Who can stand this manic pace -
The crowd.

Doors swing open to reveal
Wounded horses, broken wheel
Sounds of fighting, steel on steel
In combat.

Adrenaline begins to kick
Tortured eyes, scanning quick
Looking for some cunning trick
To survive.

Swiftly now the sword is drawn
Thrusting hard the flesh is torn
And blood red bodies greet the dawn
The gladiator.

Sylvia Duffell, Stourbridge, West Midlands

GRANDAD

You held my hand when I was young,
I remember so well, with pride.
It was firm but soft and led me along
Life's path, so long and wide.

As I grew, I appreciated more
Your wisdom and quiet dignity,
That years of experience had given you
And you passed on down to me.

Now you've gone, I cherish those times
And when, some days, I pine,
I close my eyes and I still feel
Your tender hand in mine.

Louise Green, Solihull, West Midlands

CLASSY

You couldn't, get better than our little Cathy
She is oh so slim and very classy
A real bonny petite little lassie
A strawberry blond, it's not her true colour
She is not slow when it comes to wit
Oh so full of true grit
Always out for a prank or a lark
You'd never shut Cathy away in the dark
With sea-green eyes and a cheeky grin
She'd pull you a pint or a short
She pretends to be dizzy like all blondes do
But beneath that facade
There beats a heart of gold
For our little Cathy will never grow old
She'll always be a beautiful sight to behold

Michael Nickson, Coventry, West Midlands

THE OLD MAN

Naught stirred, except a flicker of the candle's flame
As the old man slouched, in his worn-out chair
His mood was quiet, like a mouse
Stealing from the larder's fare

With no electric light or TV glow
He could see only shadows on the wall
And as the contour of the burning candle, changed
The old man worried, lest it should fall

There was an optimistic, kind of hoping
While the candle's flame was strong and bright
But the old man knew, that when it ended
He then would have no warmth or light

This was now a time for quiet reflection
Of the old man's long and cluttered life
And to remember all that gained him merit
As he coped courageously, with toil and strife

Stubborn pride, mixed with some dementia
Was aided only by a candle's flame
When the old man died, he was cold and lonely
And his neighbour's wept, with guilt and shame

Ted Phillips, Solihull, West Midlands

OUR CHILDREN

We teach our children to be independent
and stand on their own two feet.
How to tie up their shoelaces
and how to cross the street.

How to deal the the little problems
one meets along life's way
And hope that they will happily marry
and give us grandchildren some day.

So why, oh why does it hurt so much
for we know some day they will roam,
yet nothing on earth can ease the pain
when they tell you, I'm leaving home.

Margaret Wilson, Solihull, West Midlands

LET ME BE

Let me be the sunlight,
that brightens up your day.
Let me be the moonbeam, at night,
that lights your way.
Let me be the silver cloud,
that breaks through skies of grey.
Let me be the peace and calm,
that soothes your cares away.
Let me be the bringer,
of sweet dreams as you sleep.
Let me be that special place,
your love to always keep.
let me be your poem,
your sonnet and your rhyme.
Let me be your guiding light,
until the end of time.

Mike Tinsley, Dudley, West Midlands

TO MY MOTHER

The silent, fearful world you now inhabit,
Leaves me dead inside, but dutiful.
I visit every week, but do you know me?
Flashes of the old humour break through;
Then you mock your fellow residents
And insult your carers.
I leave the room, you greet my return
As if I'm just arriving.

This tragic, sad end-piece to your life
Should not erase the cheerful, generous soul that was;
And in your twilight, unknowing, you have forged
A new friendship between dad and me.
What's more, once he was resigned,
Qualities of patience, tenderness and love
From dad to you surprise me still -
In sickness and in health indeed.

Peter Hayling, Birmingham, West Midlands

Born in Castle Donnington, **Peter Hayling** has interests
including drama, psychotherapy and listening to music. "I
have been writing the occasional poem since I was 21, as a
way of expressing my inner self and my search for meaning,"
he remarked. "My work is influenced by the wonder and
beauty of nature, my faith and my family. I would describe
my style as honest and sometimes lyrical but still developing
and I would like to be remembered as someone who unique-
ly and succinctly expressed his experience of living in this
world." Aged 59, he is a book-keeper with an ambition to
express himself freely. He is married to Anna-Leena and they
have five children.

THE LAST TIME

Shadows of yesterday slip slowly through the door
Taking their memories on the way
I'm searching for light to shine on me before I go,
But giving up is giving in.

Enter my dreams tonight, and fill me with your love
Bring me laughter in my sleep
Take away the emptiness, the cold I fell within,
Give me warmth and give me hope.

Sometimes I'm helpless, but the morning seems to know -
The day it brings is like newborn spring.
The life I lead is so much more than just one show,
It's the first night and the last night alone with you.

Paul Harris, Solihull, West Midlands

I DON'T DO EMOTIONS

I don't do emotions,
Emotions are for the insecure,
So don't look at me that way,
Expecting me to say something.

When I am with you,
My barriers are up,
I've got my bullet-proof vest
And crash helmet on.

I won't feel a thing,
When you say, you love me,
Just don't expect anything,
In return,
Like I said before,
I don't do emotions.

Sabiha Ullah, Birmingham, West Midlands

ODE TO RORY

Tall dark and slender with vivid blue eyes
at six foot six, a giant, you stand high.
Tattoos and shaved head strike fear on first view.
I felt intense fascination for you
enraptured by the rhythm of your beat
love of music, timed with tapping feet.
Drum loops, guitar riffs hold strong passion,
wild youth still strong in your ambition.
To me, fierce love and inspiration,
belief in myself and tenderness too.
These must have been divine intervention
the day fate twisted and turned me to you.
We are together against all the odds
I think we are just the luckiest sods.

Claudine Weeks, Bilston, West Midlands

FISHERY CREEK

Alone I wander along its banks
Feet avoiding the black muddy pools
Seeing the brown rushes and reeds in ranks
Rising up from roots that water cools
Watching a heron ducking it's head
It feeds from the bottom of the creek
Aware of the kingfisher, unfed
That is diving down to fill it's beak
Skylarks saturate the slack warm air
With their lilting and trilling spring song
Glimpse an otter that's out from it's lair
Hearing the wood pigeon cooing so long
Strong is the calling of wild nature
Setting my fast-beating heart afire
I feel now that I am more mature
I can say to you, you are my desire

Len Beddow, Wolverhampton, West Midlands

ALL I NEED

All I need to see is you smiling,
At the start of each bright new day,

All I need to hear is you laughing,
To remind me that I need to say,

All I want is for you to still love me,
And no matter what comes I'll get through,

I can cope with whatever life sends me,
Just as long as I know I have you.

Alan Davis, Walsall, West Midlands

Alan Davis said: "I am 57 and was born and raised in
Walsall in the West Midlands. I am married to Jennifer and
have five children and three grandchildren, all of whom
have been a source of inspiration for my writing. My hob-
bies are winemaking and, of course, writing poetry. I have
been writing seriously for about three years, and have
joined *www.poetrybox.com*, a website purely for aspiring
poets. I think my biggest influences in writing are nature,
and my family, and I write to express my feelings and my
fears."

THE STAIRCASE

I'm falling again
Into this deep coma
I feel light
The air just carries me
Further and further
Down I go
Who will catch me?
Who would want to?
So I land
Hit myself so hard
The vibrations shatter
Throughout my body
I stay here until I wake

Cheri Stanbury, Birmingham, West Midlands

SILENT TEARS

In a dream last night
I saw my mother cry,
My face, a reflection
In the opaque, crystal waters
Of her dark troubled eyes.

The pools, overflowing,
Flooding streams upon her face.
I sought tender comfort,
To stem the flow of grief,
To dry her tears with lace.

But I, moving to seek reason,
To stifle unseen fears,
Awoke into midnight blackness,
To the bitter salt-sting
Of my own silent tears.

Alan Woodhams, Chelmsley Wood, West Midlands

THE NIGHT IS OURS

Come, carry me in your arms to the setting sun
Far from days dawning
Where we will find the million mysteries of the night
Without sound or sight.
Hands fashion the beauty that daytime knows not,
Lips have no need of speech.
There is a warm, soft darkness all around us.
Even the trees have melted away.
So, what matter if our bodies shine white,
For they see only moonbeams,
Left behind to taste the wonder of still soft velvet.

What, is it morning so soon, so soon?

In the distance shines our lake of happiness
Come, give me your hand.
We will run to the brink and drink
Long cool draughts
Of laughing, rippling, water, for the night was ours
And this day is ours.
There will be no parting after.

Betty Harper, Solihull, West Midlands

EMPTY NEST

My son's gone to uni,
Hope I don't go loony.
No mobile text typing,
I'd better stop griping.
No more loud rock or rave,
The house is like a grave.

I'm in an empty nest,
My youngest has gone west.
He's geared for more learning,
It won't stop me yearning.
I just hope he's okay,
He's coming home one day.

Angela Kirby, Coventry, West Midlands

SELF-PORTRAIT

I am an old-fashioned girl
With an old-fashioned hat
Just a bit about myself
To make you smile
Giggle and laugh.

Yes, hello to you
And you and you
Wish I could jump
Out my picture frame
Just to shake
Hands with you.

It's fun being a picture
I say to myself
Could be on your wall
Or on the shelf.

Julie Rowe, Wolverhampton, West Midlands

MOST EVIL

To the devil I once did see
He came in my dream one night
With his dark eyes he stared at me
I just froze and gripped the pillow
With fright.

For his head was round and green and bold
And he must have stood seven feet tall
As my name was surely called
And it echoed deeply off the wall

All he wore was a long black cape
Motionless I lay in bed asleep
For my mind he was able to rape
And implant the nightmare for me to keep

It was a weird dream
I had that very night
I don't care how stupid it might seem
It was not you who had the fright

At the time I was to read
About Alister Crowley and all his greed
But you don't play with evil like a toy
So I shut the book and said goodbye

Colin Peace, Bloxwich, Walsall, West Midlands

DYING

The soft folds and curved creases
That travel directionless down the dunes
Of your hand, interweaving with one another
And crossing like estuaries over land.
Each rise and fall, each fine trace carefully
Depicted by its artist, holds meaning;
Wisdom unimparted, happiness unshared,
Beauty undescribed, experience unrelated,
Hardship untold, lessons untaught;
Hiding within the blanket of
Your hand.

Saajida Mehrali, Birmingham, West Midlands

BECAUSE OF YOU

Along life's paths, of ups and downs,
of ins and outs, of smiles and frowns.
Sometimes things happen,
that give no doubt,
as to what life's all about.

From childhood home, we must all go,
to walk a path we do not know.

To meet perhaps, a soulmate true,
just like the one I found in you.

And when the family gathers near,
children, grandchildren, all so precious, all so dear,
everything becomes more clear,
and I know, it's oh so true,
My life is enriched,
because of you.

Jacqueline Claire Davies, Dudley, West Midlands

LISA

Are you blind?
Do the birds not sing the angels' harmonies for her?
Is there no words left to find?
Mountain, nor valley, sea nor task could deter.

The wolves howl.
Devil plays diversionary games
I would hold her light by fair means or foul.
My heart with her is tame.

Steven Goodall, Willenhall, West Midlands

I'D LIKE TO SAY

I'd like to say, "I missed you."
I'd like to say, "I cared."
That I could not dismiss you
That you were always there
For me, the bell, it tolled
But not for thee, its answer
Went unheeded. I'd like to say,
"You went away, but not
When you were needed."
On one sunny afternoon,
I'd like to say, "You went too soon,"
While I was digging up the garden,
Making plans, begging your pardon.
This, and more I'd like to say
And would have done
(Not to your face)
As you were never in,
And when you were, not listening.

Emma-Louise Cartwright, Sutton Coldfield, West Midlands

THE INNOCENT

Through the eyes of a child, the innocent
What a wonderful world they must see, the
Christmas trees, the fairy lights, their land of
Make believe, and in their magic wonderland,
Everything seems right, your loving arms
Around them, your tender kiss goodnight.
I'm glad that they don't understand the hate
That's in some men. I wonder if there will
Ever be peace again.

Betty Wright, Walsall, West Midlands

MISSING

A remembrance of someone
Who is not there.
The sweet past full of memories,
Time stands still when reminiscing.

The wake of morning
Brings on the onslaught of reality,
The heart aching even more than before.

Looking through dull and cold eyes,
A person living life inside,
Living through life routinely,
Grasping onto passing opportunities.

Yet, still not at one.
Taking one day as it comes
Living life by a single thread.
This one will always just remember
The one thing that is always missing.

Nazma Ghafoor, Stechford, Birmingham, West Midlands

MY ALL

The light of my life,
The joy of my soul,
Your existence makes me whole.
The sustainer of my life,
The essence of my being,
The core of my spirit,
My root, my all, my everything,
My mother.

Tonya Bolton, Birmingham, West Midlands

EQUILIBRIUM

Suddenly I can no longer find things -
things that were never lost before.
Papers have shuffled themselves into drawers,
newspapers hauled themselves back into open-mouthed
racks.
Houseplants that were bowed, have stretched anew,
books have arranged themselves into neat stacks.

Suddenly the house has new fragrances -
jasmine, perfume and lemon floor cleaner.
Strangely, the floury sprinkling has disappeared
from window ledges and the tops of door frames.
The flaccid pillows have been plumped and fussed,
while the faces in the photograph frames now possess
different names.

Suddenly, a feminine touch has infiltrated the equilibrium,
like a wind hushing a mountain and cooling its crest.
Suddenly, I no longer have to imagine
the smell of your hair as you sleep, soft upon my breast.

Andrew Detheridge, Cradley Heath, West Midlands

I'M SORRY

I'm sorry for the pain I've caused,
My thoughts are always wrong.
Sorry for all the hurtful words I've used,
Only you could have stood it for so long.
Rage is when I wish time was paused,
Rushing words have pushed so strong.
Your heart is made of gold.

Samantha-Jane Ives, Walsall, West Midlands

DEAR ELAINE (LOVE LETTERS)

From that first day when I met you, I knew that you would be
The girl I'd love forever, until eternity
I asked you out and you said yes, my heart was full of pride
Years later you said yes again, you agreed to be my bride

We married at St Andrews in July of seventy-three
I left my home a Bromford and joined your family
After six months we got lucky we saved, bought this and that
We got ourselves our first home in a Chelmsley high rise flat

We tried for children straight away but it was not to be
It took four years of heartache until Sarah made us three
Young Eric came in seventy nine, our family now was four
We were so proud and happy we could ask for nothing more

Now thirty years have passed, our kids will soon move on
But we will still be lovers, still together, still as one

Eric C Hill, Solihull, West Midlands

MEMORIES

Memories of when we were young,
Happy days when we were young,
Peaceful days when we were young.
Now I look back at those days
Walking to school with our friends,
Happy to share our sweets.
Oh the delights of sharing, never
Minding, never expecting anything in return,
Just glad for friendship and laughter.
Those were the days I shall always
Remember, for the rest of my life.

Kathleen Gee, Leicester, Leicestershire

FLEUR: EPISTLE

Dear Fleur,
If there is a girl who can make me stare
For years into the abyss of our street
And peer round the corners
Of every neighbour I meet,
Half-listening to what they are saying -
Silently praying - you'll return in minutes:
Or can make me admire (but not enquire)
About the smoothest, straightest legs in history:
Or can make me dream both
Asleep and awake and get poor Richter
To quake deep inside;
To watch this electra glide
Down the road on foot or bike,
Carelessly caressing the air
And setting the summer ions alight:
Oh Fleur, if there's a girl who
Can get me in such a state,
It's you.

David Copson, Coventry, West Midlands

LOVING YOU

The mighty oak should wither and die
And the seas turn to dust
That the sun no longer shines on high
As clouds no longer fill the sky

That churches shall no more turn to God
And farmers no longer plough the sod
No more will stars flicker in the moonlit sky
No more will we hear politicians lie

Rain shall stop falling and rivers flowing
Birds shall stop singing and grass stop growing
The earth will stop and time stand still
And man would lose the desire to kill

The universe would find its end and the
Leaning tower would lose its bend
No more famine, no more flood
No more hatred, only good

How much do I love you, let me count
The ways
Infinity is not enough, you cannot count the days
How long shall I love thee, until the
World begins anew.
For all this would go before I ever
Stopped loving you

Christopher M Harris, Market Harborough, Leicestershire

YOU ARE THE ONE

You are the one I look up too,
The one I want to be like,
You have been there all my life
Teasing yet infuriating, but you were there.

You are the one, who
I sometimes hate but often love,
The one who was more of a raven than a dove,
All my life you were there for me.

You are the one I admire
Older, wiser and stronger
You and I share a mother
Because quite simply, you are my brother.

Charlotte Thompson, Loughborough, Leicestershire

RUBY WEDDING

If you should ever find it steep
To climb the upward land,
Protest or not, I'll carry you.
I'll keep my ruby promises
Until they turn to gold.
To this you have my hand, I'm always true.
However old, however close to sleep.

We'll walk together over whistling sand,
As sun goes down;
And after many golden days of life,
Drown in a Welsh sea
Where all the love there is
Reborn from time on Heaven's shore
Laps yours and mine
Eternally.

Arthur Barlow, Long Eaton, Nottinghamshire

THE COLOURS OF LIFE

When you die,
Your space dies with you.
It remains as it was,
Untouched,
Yet subtly changed.
It becomes free of the colours of life.
No yellow happiness,
No blue sorrow,
No pink affection,
No red anger,
Simply a dead grey.
In a world less cheerful,
With your passing.

Alistair J R Ball, Leicester, Leicestershire

JUSTICE FOR JAZZ

I'm so sorry, I didn't do you justice did I?

Half moon question mark,
On steel planes your eyes shine out,
Dark as coal.

You grasp and twist and
acrobatically swing.

You are so sweet,
You are an escape for me,
I will never ever forget,
Just me and you,
Just me and my jazz.

Sylvie Wright, Leicester, Leicestershire

FILL THE SPACE WITH YOU

Fill your walls with posters
Fill the space with you
Fill your play with coziness
Fill your thoughts with hue

Fill your home with nice things
Fill the house with you
Fill your place with openness
Fill your work with view

Kelvin Donaghey, Enderby, Leicestershire

SHOWING MY GRANDDAUGHTER OLD PHOTOGRAPHS

And this one is my own Grandad, portrayed
In sepia shades of face and uniform
Before he sailed for France. His arms were warm
And strong: but though he held me tight and played
His Grandad games, I never could persuade
Him to reveal his stories of the storm
Which blotted out his youth. The chloroform
Of time and love had helped those memories fade;

But I needed to know: after he died
I learned the secrets he had never told.
And while I know you'll not sit on his knee
As I once did, I'll talk of him with pride
So you will know him too. We will grow old
Remembering what he did for you and me.

Dylan Pugh, Melton Mowbray, Leicestershire

WITHOUT YOU

The wind blew across the sea, sending waves of love
Rushing through my heart. There were echoes of time
Flying into the distance as the cliff walls were
Pounded and thrashed.

Where is my sweetheart after all these years, and when,
Will you get safely home? Birds cry, whales swim and
Sharks hunt. All I can do is search. Amid the
Chaos and confusion I yearn for your love. Please
Come back to me.

Life's delicate breath of peace entwines with
Happiness in my soul, as I look at you in my mind's Eye.
Your radiant smile, your piercing blue eyes
And your sculptured frame. Then, the river
Swells, the waterfall cascades and I know my love
For you is still strong.

All this time without you on life's long meandering
Journey makes me feel so alone. Is there any
Hope?
Maybe now and then. Maybe in the
Future, we can meet again.

Julie Hill, Market Harborough, Leicestershire

THANK YOU

My hopes for you are endless,
Stretched beyond your goals and dreams,
I believe that you'll excel
When everyone else is on their knees.
My trust in you is sacred
And though I don't tell you when I can
My love for you will override
The strongest passion known to man.

Jenny Lynch, Ashby-de-la-Zouch, Leicestershire

ROWENA FOREVER

Life is never what it seems
When your face devours my dreams,
A radiant laughing in your eyes
That took my poor heart by surprise.

A heart that crumbled in your hand
You are the power in my land,
When I drink the tears you cry
I'm in heaven before I die.

I wish to stand inside the rain
And always take away your pain,
Blow winds of heaven's sweet air
To caress your golden hair.

We're sinking in quicksands of time
Forever love will always rhyme,
Love is heaven and it's hell
Beside you I can never tell.

Roy Iliffe, Braunstone, Leicestershire

PA

Dad I love you but it is hard to say to your face.
You and I have an unspoken bond.
When I shake your hand and say goodbye,
I try but I'm such a macho fool I choke.
One day I will say those words that mean so much.
I hope it's not too late.

Lee Busby, Leicester, Leicestershire

BECAUSE

Why does my heart flutter
When I think of you?
Why do my eyes shine
When I look at you?
Why do my lips quiver
When I kiss you?
Why does time stand still
When I am with you?

Why do I long for your touch
When you are next to me?
Why do I hang off your every word
When you talk to me?
Why do I catch my breath
When you smile at me?
Why do I swell with pride
When you are out with me?
Why? I love you.

Michelle Ritchie, Whitwick, Leicestershire

Dedicated to David, because I love you.

MY LITTLE MIRACLE

That light in his eyes when his first smile came
I'm melting inside when he looks up at me

Those dainty little hands that cling to mine
A gift from the heavens, so cherished is he

A sacred love that can never be undone
The joy this brings me is beyond compare

I'll teach him compassion, honesty and love
And a promise for him, I will always be there

He is my baby boy and a blessing bestowed
Thank God almighty for my little miracle

Emma Stannard, Grimsby, Lincolnshire

FROM FAR AWAY

I see that water in your eyes,
And know the pain within your heart,
But I cannot help you, I am not there.

I hear the tremble in your voice,
And know the misery you feel,
But I cannot talk with you, I am not there.

I feel the shiver down your spine,
And know the fear that spreads within,
But I cannot touch you, I am not there.

I am not with you, I am not there,
I cannot let you know I care,
But I know your pain and feel your fear,
I need to say you're not alone.

Jessica Furse, Loughborough, Leicestershire

I DREAM

I dream of things I'll never see
I dream of you and me.
I dream of loving you all night
In a place we'll never be.
You are promised to another,
And will never be to me.
I dream of things I'll never see
Of us loving eternally.

Ben Scanlan, Loughborough, Leicestershire

NOTE TO SELF

What's the point in walking by?
The eternal stars in a mortal sky,
Take to the air and fly,
Look down and watch civilisations grow and die.

So what's the point in walking by?
Seize the moment,
Don't be afraid to say "hi",
Because you're only here for the blink of a star's eye.
The point again? In walking by?

So why do you live locked up from joy?
And fall for every stupid ploy?
And always act shy and coy?

You make yourself suffer, but why?
What's the point in walking by?
Go on. Go up to her, Say "hi",
And stop your forever long goodbye.

Alex McQuade, Sleaford, Lincolnshire

ANTITHESIS

The beginning was nothing like this,
Outward manifestations,
Similar, or so I thought.

Where did it all go wrong?
Momentary definitions,
What I thought a friend should be.

Now my problem is difference,
Spontaneous effects,
That tell on only me, not you.

Sophie Nuttall, Holton-le-Clay, Lincolnshire

THE ARTIST'S DILEMMA

The morning light, through the window shines,
Lighting up my canvas, prepared for my skills.
Now what shall I paint, on this canvas of mine?
A country scene with distant hills.
A farmyard maybe, with tattered old barns,
Or, a lakeland scene with rocks and tarns,
A three-masted schooner, with billowing sails
With storm clouds racing by.
Or, a still life scene, that meets the eye
Of a battered old teapot surrounded by
Apples and flowers with crusty old bread,
With backdrop, of velvet, deep red.
A portrait maybe, of a pretty young girl
Or of a nude lady, just wearing a shawl,
I've waited too long, to make up my mind,
The bright light has faded,
The sun has declined.

F J Dunn, Louth, Lincolnshire

LOST LOVE

Oh my darling I do miss you
Since you passed away
For I did love you in a very special way
My heart is now broken and there's nothing I can do.
For all I have left are the memories, the memories of you.
So to God in Heaven I will say a little prayer
Please Lord save a place for me
Next to my love up there.

Robin Morgan, Wainfleet St Marys, Lincolnshire

GOLDEN WEDDING

We've been together fifty years,
And never a single row,
I didn't believe that story then,
And I don't believe it now.

If two people live together,
And always think alike,
Think how boring it would be,
Each day and every night.

You need to have a challenge,
Each others views to compare,
And give and take a little,
To show you really care.

I suppose that I've been lucky,
And I hope that he has too,
In finding someone who really cares,
And wants the best for you.

Iris Covell, Timberland, Lincolnshire

DAISY

Golden hair
Button nose
Bright blue eyes
Pretty clothes
Singsong voice
Little smile
Breath as sweet as camomile
Darling daisy
We all adore
Love today
Tomorrow more

Michael Doughty, Sleaford, Lincolnshire

GONE BEFORE

Her face the dear, remembered face,
Her voice the one I know so well,
Her brain is the proverbial empty shell.
Here but not here, there but not there,
Speaking a language few can share.
She looks at me and sees her mum,
Long dead now, she knows me not.
She lives her life one minute at a time,
And yet she's happy in her own sweet way.
She's not aware that anything is amiss,
But it wrings my heart to see her like this.
We're left behind in this whirling world
To feel a pain she cannot know.
She smiles brightly, glad to see us go,
Seeing only fleeting glimpses of what we were,
Her spirit gone before to some strange nowhere.
The final shock of parting when she is dead
Echoes the sad goodbyes already said.

Margaret Todd, Burgh-le-Marsh, Lincolnshire

LOVE'S JOURNEY

As I look back my darling, at the journey we've travelled
All the good times and bad times, the problems unravelled
We kept on the road when our soles wore quite thin
Taking what's thrown at us, square on the chin
I have savoured each moment, held on tight round each
bend
And we've travelled together as lovers and friends
Our love has sustained us through sickness and health
For richer and poorer, we made our own wealth
We've manoeuvred our life round the twists and the turns
Now we're older and wiser, many lessons we've learnt
Enduring all weathers, sunshine scattered with rain
I'd buy another ticket, if I had my time again.

Jane Glover, Wrawby, Brigg, Lincolnshire

BUSY LIZZIE

I'm busy, busy, busy, I haven't got time to think,
I'm cleaning up the house or I'm washing at the sink.
And when it's time for bed, I cannot get to sleep,
I'm busy in the farmyard, counting up the sheep.

If retirement is supposed to be a time of rest and leisure,
I haven't got the message, 'cos for me it's not all pleasure.
It's all get up and go, do this that and the other,
And when one week's work is done, it's time to start
another.

"Go out, enjoy yourself," they say, and join the social club,
They do all sorts of things there, and luncheon at the pub.
So now, the housework's gone to pot, my dreams are way
beyond,
For the housework will still be here, when I am dead and
gone.

Elizabeth Chivers, New Waltham, Grimsby, Lincolnshire

BE MINE

Let me look into your eyes
To find the road to Paradise
And seek the ultimate surprise
Hot as fire, or cold as ice

How eagerly I try to please
To still your taunts that never cease
But passion haunts me as you tease
Please grant me merciful release

Your harsh unfeeling friends suppose
My urgent, raging passion gross
But still your vibrant body glows
Be gentle, loving, kind and close

Donald Turner, Sleaford, Lincolnshire

GOD

God, where were you when my ship was sinking?
Where were you when my lover was leaving.
You left me to drown in my own despair
Without a word or a sign that you were there

Where were you when I had no money,
No self-respect, no food, no clothing?
Tell me God if there's a purpose to your plan
Or are we all just doing the best we can

Is there a heaven, a hell, or are we deceived
By a self-created image we've chosen to believe?
God, where were you when I cried alone
Did you die, or have you gone to the retirement home?

Heidi Charlton, Boston, Lincolnshire

MY LIFE, MY LOVE

As I look back from here and now
I recollect that fateful day
When first we met and where and how
Our fortunes fused down life's walkway.
I lived in darkness 'til that time;
Peeped at life through curtains drawn
But then I felt a sense sublime,
Damascene journey; life reborn,
Through dark despair and sheer elation,
Together sharing life's cocktail,
Stronger with each inhalation
Our love has grown, a nonpareil.
So as I see you here and now
My thoughts reflect on when and how.

Paddy O'Neill, Woodhall Spa, Lincolnshire

DIY SOS

My husband's into DIY and self-sufficiency
He's so busy with a score of jobs, he hardly thinks of me.
He's always got a hammer or a garden fork to hand,
A screwdriver, a paint brush, or he's digging up the land.
We have a good supply of cabbages, potatoes, leeks and sprouts,
While indoors there are numerous shelves, and the kitchen tiles he grouts.
Just now he's taking up the boards and checking all the wiring.
"Hand me the torch," is his constant cry. It really is so tiring.
To liven up the day, I call, "John, the kitchen's all ablaze."
"Don't worry love," he answers, "I'll fix it in a couple of days."

Joan Daines, Freiston, Boston, Lincolnshire

DAYLIGHT CHORUS

The sun's warm glow, could not blaze,
As deep as my heart from your touch,
No beauty in this world could compare,
To your smile that I miss so much,

The daylight chorus up above,
Is drowned by my singing soul,
Like the sapphire sky devoid of stars,
My heart without you is not whole,

The sensations felt from the heavens above,
Couldn't hear what I feel from your eyes,
The dazzling wonders of the universe,
Are nothing compared to your guise,

The infinite hours that we possess in life,
Is how long I'd wait for you,
Nothing in this great wide world,
Could change me feeling like I do.

Mitch Cokien, Grimsby, Lincolnshire

Dedicated to Cheryl Anne McHugh for bringing the happiness back into my life. Thank you, always.

ARTISTIC IMPRESSION

The girl from the polytechnic
the student bike, names the same
Polly, spelled incorrectly, like
L extra, what's her technique
her form is magnifique.

She studies biology, human bodies
art and design, what plural of the latter
has she got on mine, no matter, her hobbies are fine.

"Come up, see my etching," she says
"Saves fetching it down."
Make note of Mae West's quote being altered
as Polly sways unfaulted, up the stairs
me in arrears, eyes dote, making note
making fuss, of posterus,
such a lovely bum
from all that male cycling.

Philip Johnson, Spalding, Lincolnshire

Born in Holbeach **Philip Johnson** enjoys listening to music
and writing poetry. "I started writing poetry when my father
died," he remarked. "It gave me a psychological therapy to
deal with my innermost thoughts. My work is influenced by
Spike Milligan and Philip Larkin and I would like to be
remembered eternally and with pride." Aged 56, he is
retired and has two children. "The person I would most like
to meet is God to ask him what the old test was and what
the new test meant," he joked. "I have written short stories
and over 200 poems, around 25 of which have been pub-
lished."

MAN OF STEEL

As a child, in awe, I watched you,
When, at bullet speed, you soared,
Over the city to rescue,
Those whom all others ignored.

And at the film's big finish,
When the bad guy had gotten his due,
I found myself left with just one wish,
To grow up a hero like you.

And those uneasy teenage years,
When I began to notice girls,
I felt more keenly all those fears,
That in midnight thoughts would swirl.

I envied you for what you were,
For what you had and knew,
Charisma, fame, a blue-eyed stare.
I wished I could be you.

It's different now, for as I grew,
I think I've learned to cope,
A crucial lesson taught by you,
To never give up hope.

Paul Hughes, Grimsby, Lincolnshire

OUR GREATEST BRITON

Bald, fat, cigar in hand,
The greatest Briton in the land.
Churchill, a man of rapier wit,
Stern countenance and bulldog spirit.
He grasped the helm when the times were bad.
Gave the world the chance it nearly never had.

His simple, measured, courageous speeches
Emboldened men on foreign beaches
And lifted hearts of wives at home,
Their lives destroyed. Simply blown
Away by a deadly rain from the night's sky.
Our heads hung low, but were lifted once more on high,
By stirring broadcasts he would deliver,
That even now, cause our spines to shiver.

A state funeral no less than he deserved
A king amongst men rightly revered.
He thanked the few.
Now we thank you.
Churchill, man of heart, head and power.
Yours was Britain's finest hour.

Patrick Smith, Grantham, Lincolnshire

SOULMATE

You brush my cheeks with rouge from one small glance,
Brief, inviting breaths against my ear,
Cause pulsing, tender nerves of love to dance,
My heart remains that vessel you can steer.

A rush of love will glide from a caress,
To settle in my deepest, inner core,
Exposed, I stand before you fully dressed,
Yet feeling naked, vulnerable, unsure.

Every day I breathe your very essence,
My life support, my oxygen, my air,
A love intense taught me many lessons,
To live it without you is my fear.

Imprisoned with romantic dreams of us,
At times I hate to greet the dawn brand new,
But then I smile and know I'm glad because,
Reality is better spent with you.

When life here ends and waves a chequered flag,
If taken first my thoughts will be to wait,
Should death be cruel and snatch you from my drag,
Grief will stop my heart, I anticipate.

Hayley Nixon, Friskney, Lincolnshire

BABIES IN YOUR EYES

Babies in your eyes: images of me;
Cupid's cameos frame in filigree
little embryos, struggling to be free.
Irised internees reflect a silent plea;
life lies in repose, captured yet in those
babies in your eyes: images of me.
Visions intertwine, what do we foresee?
Melon in the vine, seed implanted grows
little embryos, struggling to be free.
Strange affinity, pain and ecstasy;
life stirs in the womb: nimbus afterglows,
babies in your eyes, images of me.
Some day very soon babies eyes will see
something in our eyes: guardians of those
little embryos, struggling to be free.
Mirror of myself, you the legatee
of new life now formed, life that will expose
babies in your eyes: images of me;
little embryos, struggling to be free.

Norman Meadows, Wellingore, Lincolnshire

BLOOD RUNS THICK FROM THIS GUN

Blood runs thick from this gun
You had nothing to fear from me my son
The bullet is for Tommy you better run
You can run and play
You can run away
You didn't see
You didn't hear
You didn't see me standing there
Blood runs thick
Upon the scores
Armoured cars and battered down doors
Smashed window panes from the night before
When you get older find a safe place
You could be Tommy one day in the race
I could be the jackal looking your way
You have nothing to fear from me today
Blood runs thick from the end of this gun
And if your name changes to Tommy you'd better run
Blood runs thick from this gun

John Russell Telford, Grimsby, Lincolnshire

IF NOT MY LOVE

What do you want if not my love?
Has God everything for you
Right there in heaven above
That makes you want to be a monk here on earth.

What do you want if not my love?
Have you seen the devil today
Just what to you did he say
Or promise you for your loyalty?

What do you want if not my love?
That something I can never give
Just what on this earth it is
You always keep well hid.

Keith L Powell, Skegness, Lincolnshire

Keith Leslie Powell said: "I was born in Darley Dale, Derbyshire in 1952. After attending Roe Farm Junior and Derwent Secondary Modern School until the age of 15, I worked at my grandparents farm until it was sold in the late eighties. I then came to live in Skegness with my mother where I entered the poetry world by accident. As well as having a few poems published by many English poetry publishers, I have won the Lyric Prize 2000 Song Expo Benelux International Song and Culture Festival."

ASTROLOGY

Stars are out in force tonight,
The tapestry of evening stars.
Each one a shivering, silvered
Burst of light echoing until dawn.

I join them together in my mind
And create a masterpiece
Of celestial conjunction,
A nightly map of myth and time.

She too sleeps under this sky.
Her eyes may gaze at this same
Velveteen sheet of heaven,
Rich in its depth, majestic in its silence.

One day we will watch
This panorama of night together.
The physical distance that lies between us
Will be the substance of fiction.
Arm in arm, heads resting
With weariness abandoned,
We will view this starlit expanse
And consider ourselves the luckiest ones.

Daniel Stannard, Kettering, Northamptonshire

MY LOVER MY ENEMY

My life is yours
When you smack me down
You take another cry
This time where I lie
I pray to myself I hope I die
Vulnerable me
Can't you see that I bleed?
My heart is torn
When your tyrant fist knocks me to the floor
Oppressor
Depressor
I hate to love you

John Davies, Kettering, Northamptonshire

LULLABY

Your mouth, when you are coasting down to sleep
Has two small commas, one on either side
Sweet cusps where you have sent your smile to hide
While you lay drowned in love's fulfillment deep.
Although you do not know, my fingers creep
Across those reservoirs, then I with pride
Remembering all the rules we have defied
Touch with my lips and feel your heartbeat leap.
Breast against breast, the sheet a tangled heap
Your lashes on your cheek, my eyes still wide
I summon slumber's deepest flowing tide
Lest, wide awake, my joy might make me weep.

No, do not stir. As yet I have no right
To make you dance all day and love all night

Diana Cockrill, Bugbrooke, Northamptonshire

SAD THOUGHTS

Oh, for an hour, from long ago,
When we walked by the shore
And the tide was low!

I remember the time I spent with you,
When hearts were kind,
And love was new.

Fifty years have passed, since then,
Such days that will not come again;
Oh, for an hour, from a time long past,
But a love affair, that could not last.

Margaret Whitworth, Rushden, Northamptonshire

BROTHER

The years we shared, those precious memories,
Mislaid for eternity, behind the shadow of our childhood
innocence.
Our strong, fearless brother,
Never a day, shall I forget your cheeky fair demeanour.
Today and all our tomorrows, Graham only inhabits our
dreams,
Within the hours of tranquil sleep.
Peace be with you brother,
Let the weight be lifted.
Pray you be clothed in warm loving light,
Drifting serenely, down the cosmic river of time.
Final journey,
Bound for the ultimate freedom.
Perpetually embraced inside
The divine reposing seas.

William Milligan, Corby, Northamptonshire

COWSLIPS

Thorough the press of last year's dead grass layers
Among pricking blades, sharp spring's green spears,
A wan green mound, a livid heave appears.

The swelling mass stands paler than our dead;
Differentiates, becomes a braid of downy threads,
Each with dumb effort dragging up a pallid head.

Cowslips come again, puffed dead fingers stood in random
knots.
Each cluster runs up its resurrection smock
From which hang down bright custard dots.

Steve Blyth, Roade, Northamptonshire

LOVE LETTERS

Written when love was first declared,
And time together precious, but often shared.
So words, in public, must be limited:
And touch inhibited.
Thoughts written that could not be said
Read in private and again, reread

But written so very long ago.
Why are they treasured so?
The characters less vivid, a little faded
The leaves of paper creased, and somewhat jaded.
The envelope is crumpled and has several tears.
All marked by many passing years

But this is where their value lies.
Signs of age do not divert the eyes
from the enduring love they represent:
As strong now as when they first were sent.

John Howlett, Daventry, Northamptonshire

TRANCE

Her husband was tended with the care
She gave to folding clothes.
She wrote poetry in the blue hour,
Before her children woke.
Was this therapy?
She had a bad dad
And revelled in her neurosis
Death was an art
To be executed in the most lavish manner.
It was acutely real.
Her suicidal drive was exemplary, peerless, potent.

David Wareham, Kettering, Northamptonshire

FOR PATCH

Our love struck like a lightning bolt
In the middle of a starless night
But unlike the thunderstorm
It lasted to see daylight

We never thought love would come so fast
Or would prove to be so strong
But darling we both knew
We'd been waiting for so long

Between us we found a freedom
That together we could share
With a million miles of open road
And the free wind in our hair

You cannot live without a reason
Or love without a cause
You came and gave me both
And I'm proud to say I'm yours

Jacqui Hancox, Daventry, Northamptonshire

ROSEMARIE'S BOUQUET

Blue tella-tellerium
Grew a sweet-allurium
Of jade, if I may
To a floral bouquet

Muse-ami an aria
Rosemarie a-tsaria
And gold, if I may
To a floral bouquet

Ode,
Chorus colorevich
Sing monamourevich
My heart on display
To a floral bouquet

The odour dispenses
To sweeten my senses
The molonon-luminez
Of a floral bouquet

Richard Rochester, Raunds, Northamptonshire

COLDLY CLANGING CHURCH BELLS

Coldly clanging church bells
Driving through the rain
Creamy elderflower blossom
Sandwiching some June afternoon
Between rains
Coldly clanging church bells
Christening Sunday
Into a world of chains
Brainless iron bells
Forging links of unknown destiny
Coldly clanging bells
She is born
A girl unfurls
Flagship of our heart
Driving us
Coldly clanging bells
Wherever she goes we know
Some June afternoon, between rains
When we're gone
She'll go on

Mary Ricketts, Wellingborough, Northamptonshire

JACK'S LETTER

I have set the alarm for eight.
Put a warm bottle in your bed.
The milkman's note is by the gate,
I have done all the things you said.

I have now found those missing socks
Under the cushions on your chair,
The kitchen sink no longer blocks,
Your room is fresh with sweetened air.

I have fed the tropical fish,
Brought the geraniums inside,
I have washed every cup and dish
And the furniture gleams with pride.

The dustbin is out by the road,
And the shed in the garden, locked.
The vegetable plot, I hoed -
And the food cupboard is well stocked.

I have an appointment tonight,
And I doubt that I shall be back.
Just for you, this letter I write
And the flowers of course -love Jack

Graham Smith, Kettering, Northamptonshire

SOULMATE

I cannot believe you are gone
For I seldom noticed you there
But you were never far away,
You were always there, to care.
I took your love for granted
And gave little in return,
It wasn't till I lost you
That I began to learn,
The true worth of a faithful heart
Unselfish to the end,
I miss you more than words can say,
My soulmate, my best friend.

M S Reid, Corby, Northamptonshire

CANDLE GLOW

To the fire that burns on their mouths
that helps illuminate the path
Here's to those who know that a single pebble
creates ripples in many ponds.

To those who don't just explain, but
whose words bring the page to life.

To one white haired man whose passion
for his work was a spark for many,
and his great love of books an inspiration.
In sadness for loss but overwhelming joy for life
Your ambition was achieved,
a closeness unmatched on this earth.

Here's to you who we laughed and cried with.
To those who leave, but when they go
leave us behind their candle glow.

Frances Bowman, Mansfield, Nottinghamshire

THE DAY THE LIGHT WENT OUT ON THE WORLD

Now, guided only by the faint light of stars,
nights are harder to travel through, to get through.
The ease of it, with the moon to guide is gone.
The days sun, the radiant beauty vanished,
and I, left with a space, a hole in the heart of the sky.
Filled by memories, pictures never to be renewed or
replaced.
To remain the same for my life to come.
The dark days, the nights, an endless reel of sorrow.
I try to get by with merely a candle of thought.
Nothing, to the light you brought.
You; the light by which life could turn.
The sun and moon for all.

Kirsty Timmins, Retford, Nottinghamshire

WHAT TEARS WE'VE SHED

What tears we've shed, what eyes we've dried
And, oh, how many times we've cried;
When we are young, when we are grown,
There is no way we can disown
That inborn weakness we deride.

We cry as babes with needs denied,
As little ones when parents chide,
When young for things we wish we'd known,
What tears we've shed.

For pain when love's unsatisfied,
In private grief we weep inside,
For wretchedness when love has flown,
For sunset years we'll spend alone,
But then, in laughter, joy and pride,
What tears we've shed.

Hilary Cairns, Retford, Nottinghamshire

JOHN

The love that we shared
It was worth more that gold
It bound us together
Until we grew old
Now you are gone you are still in my heart.
The memories are there and always a part
Of the years spent together, how could I forget
The good and the bad times, the sorrow and regret
Still shining right through all the sadness and pain
Was the deep endless love that won't come again.

Phillipa George, Beeston, Nottinghamshire

Born in Southampton, **Phillipa George** enjoys driving, reading and writing. "I started writing poetry in my extreme grief after the death of my husband, John," she explained. "My work is influenced by the things I see and hear and my style is natural. I would like to be remembered as a sincere person." Aged 79, she is retired and has children Valerie, Rosemary and Angela. "The person I would most like to meet is Maeve Binchy because I love her books and she sounds like a very nice person. I have written hundreds of poems and had several published."

ADDICTIONS

I know it's there, the biscuit tin, in the cupboard;
Lurking, tempting, waiting.
All those shapes and sizes;
All covered in chocolate
There's dark chocolate, milk, even white,
Which I don't really like; but I'd eat!

So what about the diet? The cabbage soup I made today.
Well, it's not a patch on the tea-time assorted.
I'll put them all out on a tray,
And begin the diet tomorrow,
When I've demolished the wafers and shortcake.
Who says I'm addicted?

Sandra Benson, Oakwood, Derbyshire

ORANGE AND GREEN

Now Mr Paisley
you seem a jolly chap to me.
Now tell me true,
does God wear boots?
Now Mr Paisley
you have a lovely accent.
Now tell me true,
does God speak like you?
Does God sit in his Heaven
with a stern chin?
Is Mary shut in her room?
Now Mr Paisley
you seem a jolly chap to me.
Now tell me true,
does God keep a gun in his cupboard?
Are all the green eyed girls and boys
Sinners?

Derek Hughes, Newark, Nottinghamshire

COMMUNION

Seeming a soul alone
on silver-surfacing sea
shimmering with moonlight.

Time; earliest morning:
Place; the sea.

Waves, currents, moving silent on this image-sea
and shaping, sharing, caressing this soul.

Common chord of situation and soul
Can be the utter desert of sea;
the breaking, lapping loneliness.

A communing of a lost soul
with loneliness.

'Tis the exploring mind of oneself
seeing in mind's eye an image
in his self-soul-sea-scape.

John Hopkins, Newark-on-Trent, Nottinghamshire

DUET

The mighty rushing curtain of water,
Plunges downwards,
As it has for thousands of days,
Singing noisily,
The sunlight highlights its fleecy spume
And frothy, stingy spray,
Turning it for a moment into a
Magnificent touchable rainbow
As it cascades down, down, onto the
Stones and boulders lining the way.
Down, to the profusion of colour,
To the wealth of wild flowers that
Cling among the greens of moss and ferns and
Trembling trees, bordering the dark, dank pool
Lying in wait to stop its play.
The breathtaking intentness
Of the waterfall's roaring power,
The shock of contrast
At the sudden stillness,
The calm, the absolute peace
Of a gentle summer's day.

Doreen Roys, Retford, Nottinghamshire

FRESH-TURNED

"Where the earth is freshly turned
The poppies grow," the farmer said.
So that is why Flanders fields blew
Blood red in the wind.
Earth was freshly turned, oh yes,
Freshly turned and blessed
By unsung, unwanted heroism.
Mud-soaked, desperate, homesick
Men, fighting in a fog of unknowing
Hopeful, hopelessness for a land
They loved, for folk they loved,
Who loved them and who would
Never greet each other home again, in love.
Seeds sown, for peace and freedom, poppy red.

Elizabeth Morris, Kettering, Northamptonshire

JL

Give peace a chance
That's what he campaigned for
Power to the people
And a future without war
A millionaire with a conscience
Who showed contempt and pity
A superstar in Liverpool
A dreamer in New York City
Imagine He's still with us
It's not so hard to do
We could play more mind games
Milk and honey too
A reluctant icon some might say
More popular than Jesus? Never
Yet we all joined in when he sang
Strawberry fields forever.

Tasmin Hembery, Bridgwater, Somerset

MARY LOU

I'll bring you a rose,
A sweet-scented rose,
A red one that's speckled with dew.
Along with the rose,
I'll bring you my love
It's for you, Mary-Lou, just for you.

I'll sing you a song,
A beautiful song,
With lyrics you can't misconstrue.
For in the refrain
I'll repeat yet again
That my love is for you, just for you.

I'll write you a poem,
A tender love poem,
For love is my life, through and through.
It's beyond understanding,
Absolute, undemanding.
It's for you, Mary-Lou, just for you.

George Shipley, Mansfield, Nottinghamshire

BEHIND HEAVEN'S DOOR

Locked in my soft warm sanctuary
Away from prying eyes,
I reach across to where you lie
And then I realise,
The hollow where your body lies
Will be the same no more,
For you sleep with the angels
Behind Heaven's golden door.

I reach out for your pillow,
Bring it in real close,
Squeeze and fold my arms around it
In an everloving pose
As I close my throbbing, aching eyes,
Your fragrance folds around me,
To sleep the dreams of memories
And feel your love surround me.

As morning cruelly awakes me
The scent is not so strong
But love and never fading memories
Will linger like a never ending song.

Ann Carratt, Worksop, Nottinghamshire

I WOULD IF I COULD

You said you wanted me there, to give you a cuddle and a
hug,
And to wrap you up snug,
As a bug in a rug,
Well I would if I could.

You want me to go to the doctors, and tell him what's
wrong,
With you and your child;
Why he's sometimes so wild,
Well I would if I could.

To help you through your tough, hard life,
Through the trouble and the strife
Of a mother alone;
Turn a house to a home,
Well I would if I could.

I think you want me to restore your faith in the human
race,
By doing right by you,
I think it's true:
Well I will if I can.

Mark Orchard, Radstock, Somerset

MY MAN

He thinks he knows me well, my man
at times that's true to say
but something holds me back and then
I'm just a breath away
He treats me with such love and care
that I'm afraid to stay
that tempting gods of fate will bring
chaos along the way.

He is my lover, friend and mate
he fills all of these roles
when he's not there to share with me
I'm only half a soul.
I hear his footstep, hear his laugh
his voice so warm and true
the hours shared, the memories stored
within my heart to view.

I cannot think upon a day
that he's not close to me
wrapped up together, one as one
a never-ending we.

Hilary Malone, Cottesmore, Oakham, Rutland

CALMER RIVERS

I write as you lay sleeping,
early morning dew is weeping,
its tears are crystals with the frost,
and all I want to say is -
I write as you lay dreaming,
voices in my head are screaming,
a silence that I share alone,
and all I want to say is -
there are no words to show
how much I need you,
you give me space to grow
and a chance to lead you
away with me, to the moon
and calmer rivers, soon.

Nadia Martelli, Derby, Derbyshire

THE PERFECT DAUGHTER

You were my daughter,
Although I have none.
In dreams I could alter,
New wishes were fun,
You could have been mine,
You have habits like me.
your eyes and hair does shine,
for all people to see,
You were the girl,
I would have wished for,
Like a sweet, silvery pearl,
Would I ask for more,
The jokes and laughter
Will sing ever after,
You'll always be mine,
My brother's daughter.

V A Shardlow, Weston-super-Mare, Somerset

THE OLD ONES

Yes his skin is brown and wrinkled, like the bark on a
grand oak tree
And his fingers long and twisted
As only workers' hands can be

But there's warmth in his touch, a strange strength and
reassurance
That hint of pride and dignity, that lived in those, from
years gone by

And yes, his limbs are stiff and painful, the rust its name is
age,
And though his hair is stark white, thinning,
It's not yet time to leave life's stage

Because his eyes still shine with wisdom, and his mind still
holds the key
To the knowledge gained from the mistakes
Of those lost to history

But of that generation, my grandfather's the last
And the memories through which others lived
Will die with him, as he fades into the past

Eilise Lindop, Wirksworth, Derbyshire

THE PIANO TEACHER

My first piano lesson,
Eight years old,
I listen as the teacher's hands
Glide across the keys.
The music swells, filling the room
I share my teacher's joy
A spark kindles within me.

Summers fade to autumn,
My pieces get more difficult
Patiently she guides me,
Calm, encouraging,
Full of warmth and kindness.

Now, I stand upon the doorstep,
Stepping out into a new world.
School days are passed.
I listen as my teacher
Smaller now, and older
Plays her dear piano.
The spark she kindled has become a flame,
The lasting joy of music that she gave.

Edmund Hunt, Matlock, Derbyshire

FOR YOU

I miss your voice, your tender touch,
Your smile which meant to me so much,
I miss your whistling out of tune
When you walked back into the room
I miss my early morning tea
The sound of football on TV
I miss the way our hands entwine,
The magic when your eyes met mine,
I miss you for your sense of fun,
Your goodnight kiss when day is done
I could go on for evermore
To tell you what I miss you for,
I talk to you but you're not there
I find that very hard to bear,
So sleep my love without the pain,
Till we are back together again.

Edna J Insley, Littleover, Derby, Derbyshire

GREGOR THE GIANT

Gregor the giant was big for his size.
He'd two flappy ears, but only one eye:
He bellowed, and roared like the wind
from the west,
And eating up children was what he liked best.

Unfortunately, Gregor's no longer around.
He just disappeared without even a sound.
For mothers love children. They can't
be a feast,
For a bellowing, roaring, one-eyed great beast.

Carol Underwood, Bolsover, Derbyshire

For Natalie, Sophie, Laura and James, with thanks for the joys you bring to my life.

RHAPSODY IN PRAYER

Make me a melody,
titillate my senses,
instill in me ecstacy,
ravage my soul.

Make me endure
the naked flame,
the exquisite torture
of unrequited passion.

Make me to dance
in gay abandon,
gathering garlands
to place at your feet.

Make me a casket
of the world's tears,
a fountain of healing,
a pathway of peace,
the sacrifice complete.

Beryl Johnson, Cambridge, Cambridgeshire

YOU

You haunt my dreams.
You absorb my mind.
My heart is under your spell.

You are always there, in my head.
Sometimes I wish,
I wish you were dead.

I loved you then, I love you now.
I only have one question.
How?

Can we be together?
I cannot see a way.
Our future will not be as one.
You are the moon, I am the sun.

But remember this, in times to come,
For me, you are the only one.

Rebecca Bromham, Peterborough, Cambridgeshire

ART

Beethoven came and planted huge trees in my garden,
But they were quite unlike trees I had ever seen:
Such deep roots and profound branches
And leaves so light that thought stirred them.
What sort of gardener labours like this?
Is he a freak of nature - a scientific statistic
accounted for by probability?
No: he is a gardener for God
Singing to us that fruit hangs loudly at the boughs.

Alistair Morgan, Peterborough, Cambridgeshire

LOUISE

The door creaked
As I opened it.
I stepped into
The darkened room
As if by impulse
Or curiosity.
In one corner was
A flickering candle
In the other a
Woman on a bed.
The woman was old and young
Depending on how the light
Caught her.
I gently closed the door
And tried to erase
The image of what I had seen.
But the visage remained
Etched in my mind.

Timothy Jones, Cambridge, Cambridgeshire

TO CAROL

Beneath a tree in Cyprus
My daughter sings.
Is she a fairy
Spreading her wings?

Anemonies in fields,
Stony and wild.
Sunlight in the hair
Of my fair child.

Lithe is her body,
Laughing green eyes,
Gathering flowers
With honeyed cries.

While Aphrodite stands
Abashed in spume
Carol is the sylphid
Of leaf and bloom.

George Payne, March, Cambridgeshire

SCATTERED MEMORIES

I stand amongst the whispering trees
Stare unseeing at the fallen leaves.
Your voice echoes from so long before,
Before life closed you outside its door.

Your words "It's just a bit of a puff,
I'll stop when I have had enough."
The leaves seem to rustle with the sound
of raining tears upon the ground.

You said, "Mum, it's just a bit of weed."
Then followed soon a bit of speed.
"Don't worry I can stop any time!"
Back then believing every line.

Too late you felt the needle's push
Seduced again by the sudden rush.
One day, you knew it all too late,
This quest for what? Had sealed your fate.

"I love you," I shout to the unhearing trees,
"I miss you," the words are lost on the breeze,
Here seeking solace, there's none to be found
Just memories scattered with leaves on the ground.

Linda Cleveland, Ely, Cambridgeshire

FRANK BEING WASHED

Frank being washed drools like an idiot
Spits pips like a dried-up damson
The snow of eighty winters sits on his head
Around him the nurses hover
Like birds waiting their prey
Each move he makes a concatenation of pain
Like a matchstick man crushed by a child.

You tell me you grew flowers, vegetables too
You won all the classes at the local show
Beetroot, chrysanthemums, runner beans
Marched over your land
You were summer and harvest
To friend and neighbour.

Child Frank, when will be
Your next sowing or harvesting?
Across your land the petals lie
Yellow as sulphur, red as garnets
Or drops of blood -

And I cannot tell.

Rex Collinson, Cottenham, Cambridgeshire

MY INSPIRATION

You were there when I needed you
Through the happy times and the sad.
You were my inspiration,
No matter how little we had.

It's kind of hard to say these words,
So much easier to write them down.
You know if I could,
I would turn time around.

So thank you for forgiving me,
Let's begin again.
I couldn't live without you,
My inspiration, my friend.

Farrah Sassani, Ely, Cambridgeshire

FOR ALL

For all the first lessons,
First glasses of wine.
For the treats
For the gifts
For all the smiles
For making it worthwhile
For the ballet shoes
For the dreams
For the hugs
For the looks I inherited
For the friends
For the experiences
For the patience
        Thank you.
I love you. But being me, I don't know how to show it

Maria Benedicta Ward, Ipswich, Suffolk

MISTRESS IN CALICO

Dark falls the night
Against the pale of skin
As she quietly lifts the latch
Embraces and lets him in

Worried eyes in earnest
Glance back along the street
Two hearts in fear are beating
In lovers who should not meet

Auburn hair in flourish released
From silken ribbon held high
To migrate across cream calico
Russet apple of his eye

In gaslight came their passion
Between lavender laundered sheets
That held in check so long
Once spent it soon reheats

Twilight will soon come creeping
Over Victorian chimney stacks
Lace curtains will soon be twitching
Love in tryst must cover its tracks

Ian Finch, Ipswich, Suffolk

IN YOUR ARMS

In your arms is where I am happiest,
In your arms is where I want to stay.
In your arms I feel I belong,
Oh, to be in your arms every day.

I kiss your face with my fingertips,
Bathe in the warmth of your eyes.
Listen to the thump of your heartbeat,
Fall asleep with the breath of your sighs.

In your arms I am immortal,
In your arms I can do anything.
In your arms bliss is a blanket,
Just being there makes my soul sing.

I gaze at your face as you're sleeping
Your beauty makes me want to cry.
I thank God for Him giving you to me,
Without you I would just want to die.

In your arms I feel my heart flutter,
I soar like a bird up above.
In your arms I am saved from all troubles,
In your arms dear, for you are my love.

Lee Mummery, Lowestoft, Suffolk

REACH

Somewhere in the cloudiness of my mind
I had left your image
but your energy instantly knew and reached out
and softly touched my thoughts
I know you
As you elegantly sat crosslegged on a seat meditating
between wisdom and knowledge
with a presence that floated in beauty
on the stillness of noon's warmth
Eagerly in wait for a love poem
Asking "Are they sloppy", love is heavy
as you try to conjure-up the words before they were ready
in along to hold a love, half lost in the dance of childhood
running through everyday as life grow-up
skipping in the smiles you see in their innocent eyes
and the closeness of a tear
A single parent but a mother to the whole community
with a glimmer in her eye she sees hope
in this tangerine world

Paul Fisk, Ipswich, Suffolk

*For Nina, whose presence and inspiration makes this world
a little brighter.*

IN APPRECIATION OF LAURIE LEE

He opened up a world to me
Of lazy country days
With rainbow scented flowers
Where sheep forever graze

Starting off in childhood
We follow as he tries
To make sense of the world around him
Seen through a young boy's eyes

Each season brought it's pastimes
As boy grew into man
In step with nature's rhythm
Since village life began

To a London child it seemed
A distant fantasy
The fields and trees were out of reach
Just concrete blocks for me

I longed to be a country girl
Ruled by village lore
But those horse paced days of Laurie Lee
Alas, they are no more

Jackie Johnson, Needham Market, Suffolk

MY DARLING

My darling I love you
I always will

Dream of the days you
Never stood still

For you love to dance
And I love to play

On my grand piano
Every day

We make a couple
Always in love

Light by the stars
Shining above

We will walk in the moonlight
At the end of the day

Then all our troubles
Will pass away

Dennis Theobald, Bury St Edmunds, Suffolk

WNTD:

Wntd:
A gd lookin prince up 4 a larf. Must come with palace,
servnts and parnts in high places.
RSVP to Rapunzel, Merryweather Castle, Far away.

Sarah Eden, Stowmarket, Suffolk

TOGETHERNESS

Toes upon the sand,
Laughter the only sound,
Come lay with me,
Let the wind caress your skin.

Sitting by the tree,
A silent kiss,
None has looked more amazing,
You glow in the moonlight.

Take my hand,
Let your heart speak,
The tone of your voice makes me tremble,
You are so refreshing.

There is a magical feel to this day,
You exhilarate me with all you say and do,
I am defenceless, at your mercy,
I pray you treasure these moments too.

Sarah Elsdon, Lowestoft, Suffolk

EARLY TEA, MORNING VIGNETTE

Wilson brought the tea.
With a knock like thunder and feet that would wake the
dead,
Stood by my bed.
"Thank you Wilson," said I, and his grin sliced wider,
"Thank you for bringing the tea, but where is Abadai?"
"Eh, Eh, Abadai
Is sick, sick, sick,
Abadai is close to die.
But I, I have brought the tea. I, even I."
And he went,
His face aglow with his wonder of achievement.

Joyce Barton, Beccles, Suffolk

MEDUSA

Beautiful princess of Libya
How they berate you
Now, frozen in time
As the snake-haired beast
Who turned men to stone.
They didn't know you at all.
Princess medusa, how I weep
For the misunderstanding
That imprisons you, alone.
Like me.
I can see your spirit
Glowing like snow
Am I the only one who hears your cries
Of injustice?
My magnificent medusa.
Sleep well.

Belinda Budgen, Ipswich, Suffolk

LOW SELF-ESTEEM

Although recognition wraps you in its wings of comfort
You refuse to offer a platter of theories to analyse
The fortress of contrived anonymity you've built around you
Secures the stage for your theatrical disguise
Connoisseur of impenetrable expressions to mislead
A constant stream of emotion to blur exposure
Fear of rejection hides you behind cold iron bars
Where safety and isolation feed your composure

Gina Arnold, Haverhill, Suffolk

TOGETHER AGAIN

In my heart he'll ever be
He has become a part of me
And yet we two have never kissed
He'll never know just what he's missed
He is my dream, warmth, fun and laughter
I shall love him ever after
We, who fell in love so soon
Crazily in love, over the moon
Could not touch and must not kiss
Secretly, we hated this
Could not tell each other so
instead of "dearest" just a "Joe"
Me and you, so glad, so true
I'm happy you're a poet too
All constraints to four winds hurled
Now we are free to tell the world

Bryony, Ipswich, Suffolk

FILIAL VISIT

Why do I visit
When you are not there?
Although you left long ago
I stroke your soft hair
And hold tight to your hand
As you once held mine.
I stare at dull eyes
To search for a sign,
A spark of remembrance
That you know I care.
I whisper "I love you."
But you are not there.

Yvonne Allen, Ipswich, Suffolk

POSTER CHILD

Your face, thin, dark, desperate
Assaults me with its too-wide stare
I cannot even guess what horrors
Those eyes have seen, unwilling
Young eyes like that should see
Only beauty, only glory, only good
Not starving, ugly, dustbound death

So I'll scrape my purse to try
To give you what you should have
Because that would be only
Just for you

Sean O'Brien, Bungay, Suffolk

123

LIFE'S TOO SHORT

Are cream plastic handbags compulsory?
are bri-nylon cardis a must?
does beige and ecru, from raincoat to shoe,
hide a southerly migrating bust?

Are perms and coachtrips part of it?
white sandles when weather is fine.
fading gently into the background,
taking pills with Sanatogen wine.

But girls, there's still time to kick over the traces,
for adventure - for having a laugh,
try Morocco, Peru, the West Indies
or even try sharing a bath.

Be happy, enjoy life, you've earned it,
and remember to be a disgrace,
wear large earrings, and leopard-skin trousers,
not ones with elasticy waists.

When your family think you're demented,
swapping your old ways for new,
there's one thought that's really a comfort
that one day they'll be old too.

Diane Stevens, New Buckenham, Norfolk

THE GIRL THAT SENT THE ROSE AND DAWN

Thou wavering sunlit beads of rain on rose
each tear a prelude to the struggling dawn
you smile in soul of ruth that overflows
my heart with blood of love and wandering scorn.

You leave my garden thrilled, my streams elate
all fruits in flower and rainbows flourishing
till silently the morning peals like spring
and rhymes a tone of light upon our fate.

Athena's heart is bound upon the bourn,
the tumbling runes of Cronus in the breeze
they drum a cool discordance, forlorn
whilst you for me succour thrice more than these.

And yet, for now, this life's for me no more
my breast sojourns in dark and watery store
the mumbling oceans call me to their breath
and sing in Neptune's choruses my death.

Mark Andrews, Norwich, Norfolk

ANNETTA

When the fall of night
Dissolves the shadows all away.
When the cares and worries of the world
Can be forgotten for another day.
Then you and I in soft embrace
Will turn to face each other
With a kiss, and say.
"I love you".

Peter Day, Diss, Norfolk

LIVE FREE OR DIE

Migrate with me to the undersea desert
And let the sea dogs be our slaves
We can watch the shorebirds from our reef bed
See their shadows fly over and we fathoms below will live
free or die
A skiff will come and bring us whisky and sweets
And we will share them with the sea life
Floating markets will migrate our way
On the trade winds and on the white veils of surf
They will sell us sugar, beer and tools
In exchange for pearls and conch shells
And we will irrigate oil sinks
And we will weave seaweed baskets
And collect star fish to sell to passing tourists
Sport fishing men with harpoons and nets will not snare us
We will live deep
Deep under the rocks where the coral blooms bud
We will quilt the fathoms with our pasture

Natalie Knowles, Sheringham, Norfolk

THE OLD MAN ON THE STEPS

I found him sitting on the steps
Of the town's war memorial.
The town had come to life again
After the solemn silence of
Love, respect, remembrance.

"Nice place to sit," he said,
Stone warm against his back,
"Just sitting and remembering."
"Them?" I asked and pointed at the names -
That list of names and yet more names.

Not today, those friends of long ago.
No, one who had loved them too.
"Her." He pointed heavenwards and,
Eyes clouded, he looked away,
"I fought for her, and glad to.
My grandad said 'end of an era'
When the old Queen was buried."

Will MY grandchildren remember
When I tell them of the day
The old Queen was buried?

Georgina Treeves, Sidmouth, Devon

IN LOVING MEMORY

How can I perceive
The mischievous alchemy of love?
I only know that I loved you.
How can I embrace
The enfolding mystery of love?
I only know that I held you.
And when alone I huddle
Through winter nights and days,
I feel your warmth, my eyes reflect
The comfort of your gaze.

And when I heard
the overtures of spring,
I sang a rhyme for you,
And walked where once we walked
Down blossom lane,
To catch the scent of wild flowers,
And from their beauty fashioned,
A posy in the morning dew
To lay upon your lonely grave,
I picked them just for you.

Ray Coleman, Paignton, Devon

FOREVER FRIENDS

Life is never perfect,
For both a lesson learnt,
Friendship will never ride a perfect wave,
To remember the past,
Will guide us in the future,
To build a stable base on which to stand,
Whatever may lie ahead,
I know I will be at your side,
As a friend still learning to live.

Sarah Godbeer, Exeter, Devon

UNFORGIVEN

I watch helplessly as each star
Is filled with blackness,
One by one, their light is extinguished,
It is you.

I know that once the rays of the sun
Would have warmed the world,
Now everything turns to ice
Under their gaze.

Once the breeze was kind and calm,
Now it howls in anguish,
Fortelling a storm,
But I know.

Each breath fills me with pain,
Every smile with dread,
Everywhere and nowhere,
You are unforgiven.

Sarah Bidgood, Exeter, Devon

SEASONAL WINDS

I have seen the gentle breeze of spring
Lifting your curly hair from off your neck,
Inviting me also to touch you there.

I have seen, in summer, when the air scarce moved,
Stray eddies blowing dust into your eyes,
Compelling me to gently wipe your tears.

I have seen the first chill wind of autumn
Whip at your shirt and stick it to your back,
As you reached up to pick a fruit too high for me.

I have seen you braced against the gale,
With sheltering arm to guide my snowy steps,
In winter when the wind was fierce and cold.

From all the winds that blow,
From north, south, east and west,
You shelter me. I know you are the best.

We have shared the seasons and the winds,
The gentle and the cruel, the sweet, the sharp.
Together we go on till all winds sink to rest.

Hazel Williams, Newton St Petrock, Devon

Born in Bristol **Hazel Williams** has interests including read-
ing, drawing, crochet, walking and poetry. "I started writing
poetry as a child," she pointed out. "I don't know why I did it,
but I have always liked verse. My work is influenced by people,
events and scenery and my style is varied. I would liked to be
remembered as a happy person. "Aged 57, she is a teacher
and has achieved her ambition to move to Devon and find a
job she enjoys. She is married to Martyn and they have two
children and one grandson. "I have written articles on crochet
and so many poems that I have lost count," she said. "Several
of the poems have been published."

SIXTY YEARS ON

I listen to the rhythms of the day,
sweet soarings of an unseen bird,
wet swoosh of wind-blown oak
and the dull roar of traffic
outside the church yard.

I walk amidst the names of long ago,
some of them died so young,
and I remember the picnic.
A green rug oasis on the lino floor
with our rations scattered around.

Lines of figures, dancing,
torn from yesterday's paper news,
instead of promised daisy chains.
Scratchy gramophone tunes,
instead of plaintive curlews, wheeling.

Window panes crying with rain,
and Alastair in a uniform,
a uniform meant for a man.
I waved goodbye at the end of that day
to Alastair, whose last picnic was pretend.

Betty Harcombe, Moreton Hampstead, Devon

JUST A WHISPER AWAY

I feel you, just a breath away,
Just a thought to convey
How much I miss you
And this thought will pull me through

Remember the promise,
We made to each other.
Whoever dies first
Will contact the other.

Today it's hard to concentrate
What shall I do, there's much debate
Tomorrow it might transpire.
I'll find a way to pass a lonely hour.

Valerie Ann Shearstone, Bristol, Avon

TO DELIUS, THE WHITE HOUSE, GREZ-SUR-LOING

I once came across your house quite unexpectedly
On the road to Fontainebleau, the sighting brief
Yet enough to stir youth's fire; in dreams now I pass
Through garden gates, climb white steps and enter.
I find the music room at last, my hand touch manuscripts,
Your piano, the beloved painting Nevermore;
In dreams I fly from fjords, from northern moors
To orange groves in the deep south, in search of you.
Returning, I see you ensconced beneath the elder tree,
Alone; in the stillness you recall long, lost songs of love,
whilst washing over you, relentless as the sea wave,
voices from the forests, the plantations, the high hills.

It is said that some still hear your music leaping, swirling,
echoing down the willow shaded river on the road to
Fontainebleau.

Eileen Fitton, Kingsbridge, Devon

MONTROSE (1612-1650)

I too have travelled in his meteor track
Burning through Scotland like a lash of lights;
Rolled the complacent Lowland levies back,
Forged tireless through the icy desolate heights.
I too have caught the irresistible gleam
That led exhausted drunkards in retreat:
The venture and the triumph and the dream -
The ebbing hope, the shattering defeat.
Following the hangman's cart, I too have known
Fury of foes to awe and pity turn:
His butchered limbs displayed in every town,
His steadfast flame eternally to burn
And light the deeds of men. He cannot die;
"A candidate for immortality."

Eleanor MacNair, Bath, Somerset

YOUR EYES TOUCH MINE

Feel me deep inside you
Like a yearning force
How I wish to live
And breathe in your air
Exalted relief promised
Like a hidden fruit
All flavours alive
All senses dancing
The sword and chalice
With candle flame
Playing about the shrine
Kneel down before me
Lured into the flames
And in the starlight
Find me
My love

Jonathan Lawson, Newton Abbot, Devon

GETTING OLD

Getting old my love
You're not here to see
Scars of life on my hands
Lines on my face
I still hear the blackbird
Singing to sooth my aching ears
He sings just for me
Getting old my love
You're not here to see
As my sight fail me
Yet your beauty remains with me
I still walk to places we have been
Though now my back bends under the strain
I feel the pain
I'm getting old my love
You are there to see
All of what is happening to your old man, me
I'm getting old my love
I know you can see
The love that remains deep inside of me

Stuart Barrass, Honiton, Devon

*Dedicated to my dear late wife Anne Lynn, my guiding light
and inspiration in everything I do in my life.*

MALAYAN SOLILOQUY

In crowded room
I now feel so alone.
Man, company in the working hour,
Is but a background
In more leisured time.
The gentler sex,
A peopled noise.
My thoughts; my very being
Transcend the ocean'd distance
to Her,
Most sensual creature,
Upon a distant shore.

Seems yesterday we lived.

John R Tattersall, Chillaton, Devon

TAKE CARE

Take care my lovely man
When I am no longer there
To hold your hand

Just remember
The tender moments we shared
The deepest love, the joy, such care

I'll always be with you
Today and forever
For memories blessed like ours
Will live forever.

Joan Kernick, Newton Abbot, Devon

*For husband Walter and sons Mark and Stephen, if
unforseen circumstances mean we temporarily part.*

135

SOMETHING MEMORABLE

Just say something memorable
They told me.

You were the first person I have had to
You shouldn't have been.

Never given an eulogy before today,
Hoped I never would.

Couldn't put into words how it felt
To lose you.

Just say something memorable
They told me.

But nothing I could say could be
As you were.

So I just said you were, well,
You.

I let everyone fill in their own gaps
They knew how.

I only had words.

Sarah Jones, Exmouth, Devon

THE FIELD WITH SLOPE

This field with slope
was where we played,
so his brother said,
we climbed the Cornish
wind shaped trees
until mother called for bed.

We rode our hand cart
at breakneck speed,
so his brother said,
no brakes no cares
and with just a prayer
we'd stop at the old cowshed.

A graveyard now
that field with slope,
time so fast has sped,
let's leave him with
his Celtic peace,
so his brother said.

Miriam Penna, Okehampton, Devon

*I dedicate this poem to my nieces Tanya, Dayna and Donna,
in memory of their father, Alan Rowe.*

FOR BRIAN

The face there in the mirror,
This grey-haired man I see,
It must be someone else in there
It can't possibly be me.

The cards all say I'm 60
I'm sure that can't be true
It only seems like yesterday,
That I was 22.

I thought one day that I'd be rich,
Well that was my intention,
Now I find in five years time,
I'll have to draw my pension.

Christine Hall, Poole, Dorset

DANCES OF LEAVING

My inside is all in bruises:
You are beating me up with silence.
I recollect I died the other day.
To wake up and die again.
Every day.
Like the tired cuckoo in a broken clock.
I burn the hope with alcohol
And spray perfume to kill the dead smell.
I would dash across the oceans,
But I am tied up with applause.
There is only one way left:
The rail has been stolen from the station.
All I can do now
Is embroid the dances of leaving.
The leaving dances.
You are leaving.

Anna Gorjatseva, Winscombe, Somerset

DAVID

When you have days of gloom and despair
Always remember, our father is there
Watching, comforting, giving you hope
That as days go by, you will be able to cope.
The terrible things which happen each day
Have no rhyme or reason, so we say,
But knowing you'll meet your loved one again
Will help overcome your heartache and pain.
Memories live on, and will always be there
You are not alone, there are people who care.
So enjoy time together, as you both grow old
And the love for your son will never go cold.

Grace Edna Tomes, Verwood, Dorset

GRANDSONS

Suddenly grown tall,
My grandsons
Smile down at me.
In new, deep voices,
They tell me
Of their plans.
Travelling with them
Has been a journey
Of discovery
And, now, we've reached
A staging post.
They go on.
I stay behind and watch
These young men
I have the privilege
To know.

Audrey Ingram, Poole, Dorset

WORTHWHILE THOUGHT

It's the little things
Just the small things
That make life rich and sweet
A bit of harmless fun, and a chore well done
Sounds of little moving feet
And to release a bit of kindness will do
A hearty cheer for one another
You will be assured, the dear
Lord will bless you

Michael Davis, Bournemouth, Dorset

THIS TIME

Today I want to fling a rope around the world
And bind it to my heart
So that I might carry it with me to the grave and beyond.

For, this day, I saw you afresh -
Though not for the first time -
And the world was a place of unbelievable colours,
Even after dark and indoors.

There was summer in my autumn;
Music in the silence;
Ambrosia in my frying pan
And laughter in everything.

I would give you a gold ring, If I had not already done so:
I would give you my life, if there was enough of it left to
please you.
Instead, I give you my love.

Ted Harriott, Swanage, Dorset

FOR JOAN

For over forty-three years now
Our lives have been intertwined
A better companion in all the world
It would have been hard to find
I don't know how long I have left to go
I'm hoping twenty odd years or so
But I trust we're together at the end
So I can thank you for being my friend.

Phyllis Henderson, Bournemouth, Dorset

RAIN SHINE

I can't see your face no-more,
Gone without a trace.

Oh what you doin' now?
Way up on a cloud,
You know you're gonna fall,
I'll watch the rain shine.

And so you had to go away,
'Cos there was nothing left to say.

Oh what you doin' now?
Way up on a cloud,
You know you're gonna fall.
I'll watch the rain shine,
And the world could fall away,
And the stars could fade away,
And the sea could run aground,
And the truth is lies we found,
I'll still be there come the time,
I'll watch the rain shine.

Martin Ellis, Poole, Dorset

FRIENDSHIP

Friendship is a gift to be constantly treasured,
Its vastness cannot be always measured
Like cloth on a roll in a shop.
Through laughter and tears and deep understanding
Friendship and love are never demanding.
As a newborn baby is to its mother.
Rely on a friend when life is grim
Friendship stands firm through thick and thin.
A sympathetic ear is all that is needed.
If you have a friendship secure and strong
Which lifts the mind and heart along,
Like the gentle breeze we cannot see
But feel it passing from tree to tree.
Be thankful that life has given you friends,
To have and to hold till your journey ends.

Ruth Rowland, Weymouth, Dorset

Ruth Rowland said: "I was born in Whitley, in the West Riding of Yorkshire, one of a large family whose home was full of music and poetry. I qualified as an elocutionist and I have London poetry society qualifications. I give talks on poetry to WI's, church organisations and secular groups. I have had many poems published in magazines and books. I thank God for my talent and the ability to use it."

TO MY FATHER

The inevitable dark deep-shaped sleep
Shown to us through nature's constancy
Year after year, is known by her.

Earth hollows, humus filled, distills
The season's leavening, empties out
The moments and all contingencies;
Explains the illusion.

Yet, when that one sleep comes,
Closing the sight forever
Upon a wintering world,
Frost clear, in particles of ice,
Tears as icicles stab us.
Stilled, we are taken unawares
Are robbed of the mourning black
Through lack of contact.
Isolated,
We cannot share the common grief.
Then stone.
Cold stone of heart defines, how brief
Is time; how far the morning star.

Janine Vallor, Bridport, Dorset

DAUGHTER OF MINE

You walk away
And take your pain
Should you look back
I'll still be here

Space is now yours
Void of all sorrow
Shadows diminish
Not part of my life

Dare I touch you
Fragile now, don't crumble
Tears rain like droplets
Falling away silently

Reunited you returned
Arms enfolding
Hope now surfacing
Quiet times evolving

Clouds now exploding
Sunshine quenching thirst
Blanket of warmth
Gently entwining now

Sylvia Wilson, Gillingham, Dorset

To my disabled daughter, who is strong and courageous, facing life with a positive attitude, while battling with painful diseases.

Sylvia Wilson said: "I was born in Bristol and am now 66 years old. I have a loving husband, two children, a son and a daughter and two grandchildren. I have had a good life, most of which, has been spent as a housewife. I have always enjoyed reading, walking, crafts and sport. I love gardening and being outdoors, which is always an inspiration for writing. I have only attempted writing poems and short stories in the last five years. It has given me great pleasure and helped me through some very stressful episodes."

PRISONERS OF CONSCIENCE

This pain and suffering, will it ever end?
Tears and fears into one will blend,
Mental images to your loved ones you send,
But why, oh why, God me?

Days stretch into nights, blacker than black,
They are wondering, will you come back?
In your endless void of time you lose track,
But why, oh why, God me?

You just wanted to live you life,
Love you children and your wife,
Didn't expect this pain and strife,
Why, oh why, God me?

Your world will soon be full of light
Pain and memories just out of sight
Hope guiding you, burning bright,
But why, oh why, was it you?

Tereza Rule, Redruth, Cornwall

THE DOUBLE LIFE

Stark, naked, yet shrouded in mystery,
Unseen, but seeing all,
All knowing, all feeling.
People are but sheep to Her,
Empty and meaningless,
Toys for her amusement.
She has an unquenchable desire,
For knowledge, for power,
Which is matched only by Her desire,
For disempowerment by the Superior Being,
She has never seen,
But still She seeks,
She seeks.

Pete Basten, Burnham-on-Sea, Somerset

DEAR IVOR

Dear Ivor, Since we spoke
I've gone completely broke.
I've had to sell the hearse
And take up writing verse.
Oh God, I've hit the rocks!
I'm living in a box.
Please send us a few quid.
Your loving cousin, Sid.

Dear Sid, I'm really sad
To hear things are so bad
We're just back from Kuwait
So sorry this is late.
June asks me to say Hi
And hopes the box is dry.
Please find enclosed a fiver.
Regards as ever, Ivor.

Jonathan Taylor, Fowey, Cornwall

THE BALLAD SINGER

You had a penchant for singing ballads
About love, sometimes unrequited

Love with its mysteries and joy
Fingertips touch with the grace of a falling snowflake
Electricity across a room flows between the strangers gaze

How we love so well the sad songs
Emotion brimming over
Romance will never die

Gail Whitson, Exeter, Devon

SPECIAL MOMENTS

There was a moment,
When you walked into the room
My heart skipped a beat
When I first saw you.
There was a moment,
when you held me in your arms
We kissed and I trembled
At our first embrace.
There was a moment,
When we made our vows
And I felt warm inside
As we two became one.
There was a moment,
When our child was born
And I cried tears of joy
For that special gift.
There was a moment,
When you passed away,
My heart missed a beat, I trembled
And I cried tears of sorrow at our parting.

Heather D Woon, St Agnes, Cornwall

THE MERMAID OF ZENNOR

In a wild swirl of turquoise and emerald jewels
the bewitching maiden of the mystic rock pools
Sits smoothing her tresses with a coral comb,
Far from the caverns of her watery home.
On the empty stand for hours she dreams,
Silhouetted by the ocean and soft moonbeams.

Her wishes in waves like the foaming tide
Are for precious white pearls and seahorses to ride.
With a fey glint of rainbows in mesmeric eyes
She waits by the beach and she watches the skies,
Till some day a mortal the cliff-path will bring
And he'll fall for the song that this siren will sing.

For her grace and allure hold a magical spell
that sailors of yore once knew only too well;
She called them to doom in her beautiful way
And lured them below where they bide to this day.
With a swish of her tail on the pale sandy floor
The Mermaid of Zennor still waits by the shore.

Cheryl Morrison, Helston, Cornwall

Cheryl Morrison said: "I live quietly, near the ocean, where
I can commune with nature and draw on it for inspiration.
Writing poetry (also under the name of Willow Welsh) is one
of the great passions in my life. C.S.Lewis once said: *People
won't write the books I want, so I have to do it for myself.*
That is exactly how I feel about my own work. But for those
who like to share in my word-painting; the second edition
of my book *To Everyone I've Loved* is available at £4.50
inclusive of postage and packing. Please call 07980 644510
for details."

DEAR SADNESS

Don't come knocking at my door
There is no room at the inn.
All the beds are taken,
Only smiling faces sleep on my pillow.
Talk of joy is the only voice
Allowed to kiss my ears.
Cold blood isn't welcome
To pump through my ears.
Warm are my heartbeats
That sing to me sweetly in my sleep.

Charlotte Rice, Barnstaple, Devon

CHARLIE

Charlie sure has been
A bright spark
His leaving will really
Break my heart

His wit, his humour
Keeps us all sane
Life will never be
The same again

Friday's bells
Make us all alarmed
But our brows are soothed
With his smiling charm

Hands on healing
He will be
Always seeing
To you and me

Sally Boyd'Robinson, Gwinear, Cornwall

ALIVE AND WITH MEDALS

He stared at his war medals;
As bright as when fist minted,
His own lustre long since tarnished;
Only tear-filled eyes now glinted.

He belonged to a generation
That sacrificed its fragile youth,
And traded it for our defence;
For freedom - and for truth.

Although a very modest man
Who accepted his war-torn lot,
He wanted the world to remember,
All the others - left to rot?

A past filled with campaigns like his,
Couldn't easily be put aside,
Though through many a tortured memory,
God only knew - how he'd tried.

Don't ever forget this brave soldier,
Who now struggles to pull on his vest,
For if you forget the alive and with medals,
You'll surely - never remember the rest.

Clive Blake, St Teath, Cornwall

REMEMBERING

I stood beneath the old oak tree,
As the sun broke through the sky,
The golden glow reflecting,
On dewdrops far and nigh,
the mist down in the valley
Gave way, revealing pastures green,
A song that echoed from the sky
Came from a bird, to me unseen.
My thoughts went back
It seemed a thousand years
When last we met beneath this tree,
And swore that our love would last, until eternity.
But fate decided otherwise
And we are now apart,
But still you always will remain
A dweller in my heart.
And when the angels call me,
To say my life is through,
My very last thought will be
I once was loved by you.

Peter Petrauske, Falmouth, Cornwall

JUBILATO DEO

Down the alleyway running ahead
Hopping and jumping with fiery winged feet,
Jacob at four, escaping from class
Lifts the sands of the day and lets them slip fast
Through the dearest small hands.

I cannot hold these fragments of joy
Winnowed on the winds of time -
Scattered with such a profligate glee,
But concentrate them to eternal truth
Flowing constantly through me
And through the dearest small hands.

J A Murtagh, Fowey, Cornwall

GUIDE ME

Dear Father
Guide me
Through this day
Guide my footsteps
Light my way
Give me peace
That I may be
Ever nearer
close to thee
Guide me
protect me
Let me be
A loving spirit
Just for thee.
Amen.

Penny Kirby, St Austell, Cornwall

MY HUSBAND

My husband is as cynical as anyone can be.
Did he learn it at his mother's knee?
He's always putting forward his points of view,
It doesn't matter if you have one or two.
He's always right in what he says
Can't see things in different ways.
As the years pass by the worse he gets
I haven't bitten off my tongue, not yet.
He's only got one point of view and that's his very own
I just sit here quietly and listen to him moan.
I must admit, sometimes I agree with everything that's said
But only when I'm tired and ready for my bed.

Pauline Bulmer, Fowey, Cornwall

THE GARDEN

The garden, green and gracious in the early dawn
The small birds come to bless the earth
The flowers bloom around me as I move
To touch the grass bedecked in summer dew.

The shadows lengthen as the daylight goes,
The golden lily and the crimson rose
Begin to close their petals for the night
And now I learn to wait with quiet delight
For evensong that chants beyond the church.

The God of nature came to me with love
And gentle creatures brought me new delight
As slowly stars and moonshine shone so bright
And jeers and tears fled beyond my sight.

Marcella Pellow, Camborne, Cornwall

FROM ME TO ME

I never used to like me, I thought that I was bad,
Until the doctor told me, I wasn't bad, just mad.

Cold comfort in his words, is that supposed to ease,
The pain and guilt and horror, that all bipolars feel?

At last I understand, the mess that is my head,
A chemically imbalanced illness, to fill a heart with dread.

So from me to me I write this, it isn't just for you,
But to every person out there, this message still rings true.

You've got to learn to love yourself, to give yourself a break,
To try and start each fresh new day, a smile upon your
face.

For only then, with head held high and sprightly spring of
step,
Will life embrace life lovers with her warm sweet living
breath.

Penelope Hornsey, Mevagissey, Cornwall

LOSS

I burn a fire in your memory
and each night sit in your chair.
I wear your slippers upon my feet
as I watch you there.
You used to kiss me good morning.
You used to wish me good night.
You laid my ancient table each noon
and danced with me in the twilight.
Now I spend each hour at the hearth
waiting for another glimpse of you.
The table's dusty. The flowers are dying.
I don't mind. I shall not start anew.

Jacqueline Urch, Bodmin, Cornwall

MY MUM

Wipe your feet upon the mat.
You must do this but don't do that.
Mind you quos and mind your pees
Don't wipe your nose upon your sleeves.
Shoulders back. Never slouch.
Sit up straight upon the couch.
Never shout and never swear.
Never run upon the stairs.
Mind your manners. Please say please.
Never give your spots a squeeze.
Clean your teeth and wash your feet.
Look before you cross the street.
Do not fidget. Just stay still.
I always loved you.
Always will.

Val Davis, Torpoint, Cornwall

CHARLES

I loved a man with soft dark eyes
With loving heart and gentle hands
He twined my heart with silken chains
As strong as iron bands

Though it was many years ago
His love is with me still
He left to me no worldly goods -
No need to make a will

He left to me a legacy
Of life, and love, and fun
And soft dark eyes and gentle hands -
Our handsome, loving son.

Margaret Cobbledick, Launceston, Cornwall

THE OTHER ME

I love the imaginary person
I would like to be,
She has learnt to play piano
She's no amateur like me.
They say I play quite well by ear
Picking up a tune is fun,
When I sit in front of those ivories
I become the other one.
I play those Christmas carols
To a choir whose voices ring.
But I cannot play if I start to sing.
I have to hear those notes,
And sing inside my head,
For if I let them out
They kill the tune stone dead.

Cassandra May Poultney, Helston, Cornwall

HEARTBREAK

She sits by the window, propped in her reclining chair.
Reads, then glances up to see if anyone's out there.
She sits by the window, she's so very old.
My dear darling mother, the memories unfold.
The never-ending love she gave
The patience, laughter too.
The comfort and the kindness were with me as I grew.
Oh mum, it breaks my heart to watch you sitting there,
Propped up in your reclining chair.
If only I could turn back all the years
Make you young and well again.
Take away your aches, discomfort and the pain.
One day your reclining chair will be empty and so bare.
One day you will no longer be propped up sitting there.
It will break my heart to lose you
But I must let you go.
I cannot bear to see you suffering
I do love you so.

Margaret Beaumont, Redruth, Cornwall

CHEAT

She thought she'd get away with it
If she was sneaky, low and cunning
To her it would be worth it
A risk well worth the running.
She'd never been caught out before
Never caught red handed
Always careful when she went
Never been found stranded.
Never at the same time twice
She never was suspected
Never took the same track twice
Her route she redirected.
He never got suspicious
Never knew a thing
Only as gunshot sounded did
In her head alarm bells ring.
This time round her luck was out
He caught her in the crime
She should have been more careful
Left it, just this time.
The bullet tore straight through her head
The chicken still in her jaw
"Got you now," the farmer laughed
As the fox's body slipped to the floor.

Lucy Wilson, Liskeard, Cornwall

THE VALIANT HEART

Thank you for leading the way - going before us
For your battle-scars are shed,
Thank you for being a lionheart, upright, courageous
For your valour warms our tread.
forgive us for staying behind, e'en for a short while.
For God's will shall be done.
Trust us to honour our pledges, learn again to smile,
For we'll meet once again, brave son.

Valentine Hammett, St Peter, Jersey

MASQUERADE

Like a shoot of adrenaline the thought wakes me with a
start
I feel sick and empty.

My first meditation of the unfolding day,
The constant scratching in my skull as the shadows
manoeuvre across the walls of my life.
Your presence is missing, disappeared without a trace.

My every fibre aches for you.
Please soothe my frustrations.

A million and one scenarios race around my mind,
Fragments from the diaries of a crazed obsessive.
Situations I believe without evidence.
The creation of these situations devours my every moment.
The frustration drives me to distraction.

How dare you leave me?
I wear a mask that deceives the world.
Within I am weeping.

Rebecca Kindred, St Peter Port, Guernsey

ACORN

I become
What I am.
Acorn to oak,
Bulb to bud
Mountain to river
River to sea
Rain into pond.
I become the whole world,
From caterpillar
To spread bright wings.
From birth to death
The change of form
Is me.
Yet I remain a silk thread
In the web of the world,
A star destined to shine
With the best that can be.
Peace
Silence within,
Ready for death.

E Gwen Gardner, St Clement, Jersey

Gwen Gardner said: "I was born in England, but live now
retired in Jersey. I have worked in several countries in
Europe with Quakers, with refugees after the war, and have
spent regular periods in the US working for an American
University. I began to write poetry at school and now I often
write it. Some is published. I have been much influenced
by Zen and practice Zen meditation, though I am a Quaker.
I am 86, much concerned about world peace, and I am sin-
gle. I have also written a children's story about a cat, *Tiggy
Twinkle Paws*."

HOW I IMAGINE HIM

Soon I'll meet him,
He is my brother,
Native of his chosen land,
A tropical paradise and sunkissed shores.

He will come walking along the beach,
surfboard under his arm,
A broad smile and body deeply tanned,
Hey, my brother, how are you?

His escapee life is tinged with happiness,
That everything is going right,
To live in a foreign land,
There could be no better environment.

Though I haven't seen him for two years,
I'll know that we get on,
to spend more splendid days,
Out in a December sun.

For now I must lament him,
Though I'm becoming ever near,
There will be some long bus journeys,
Some more days until he will appear.

Richie Eves, St Helier, Jersey

To Carlota and Rob, an inspiring brother. This one is dedicated to you.

Born in St Helier **Richie Eves** has interests including walking, reading, writing and swimming. "I only started writing poetry a couple of years ago because I needed a way of expressing myself," he remarked. "My work is influenced by people, events, situations and the environment and my style is involved, affected, interested and creative. I would like to be remembered as someone who cared and followed lines of interest to suit the individual." Aged 31, he is a gardener with an ambition to reach greater heights as a writer. "I have written short stories and several poem," he said. "My biggest fantasy is to live in a foreign community and be able to speak the language and co-operate with them."

REACHING INTO HER SOUL

Dark secrets held in the core,
Memories of heads being kicked to the floor.
Hidden amongst the waves of time,
Her life's holding on by a precarious line.
Memories of dances of a childhood dream,
Then in darts a flash, a terrifying beam.
This old lady has secrets to tell,
A lifetime of mysteries, a soul to sell.
She's brought up her child, watched it live its life,
Now she's being killed by her own bloodstained knife.
The world's spinning,
And the secrets winning.
She breathes her last breath,
And welcomes a shadowy figure, death.

Claire Shepherd, Ruardean, Gloucestershire

FIRST GRANDCHILD

One day my life exploded
Out of the blue
I didn't expect that.
Suddenly I was alone,
Alone and drowning.
Friends rallied round,
Life went on.
I trundled through the years,
Went through the motions
With only half my soul.
Time moved on,
My granddaughter was born.
I was enchanted.
I fell in love again.
I didn't expect that.

Christine Smith, Stroud, Gloucestershire

A LIGHT IN THE WORLD

Icon of the glowing screen
a living prayer.
Your hand outstretched
touching the gutter's family.

Did the girl in you
put aside relics of hoops and dolls
to walk with the poor
and embrace the sick?

Confronting the powerful
standing firm against platitudes,
your home for the dying focus
for the power of faith.

Unrelenting, demanding
insatiable guardian of the dying.

Mother Teresa.

Illusion of frailty, flesh covered steel,
barefoot lover of the untouchable.

Rona Laycock, Avening, Gloucestershire

To Dave, with thanks for your constant love and encouragement.

Born in Bangor **Rona Laycock** enjoys spending time with husband, David, walking, travel and reading. "Living in and travelling in foreign parts has always inspired my poetry as well as people, places and everyday life," she explained. "My style is fluid and changing and I would like to be remembered as someone who was honest but sensitive to the needs of others." Rona is a teacher with an ambition to complete a book which is considered worth reading by the public. "I have written short stories, novels and countless poems and had over 20 poems published," she said. "My biggest fantasy is to travel into space and go where no one has gone before."

PLEASE WALK BESIDE ME

Everything I do now is with you in my heart
and in my head.

I still see all the beauty in my daily walk along Tewkesbury
Ham
but now through a misty veil of tears.

Are you here beside me? Do you hear me when I talk to
you?
"Oh look, there's a Heron." "Listen to the Robin."
"Isn't the sunset wonderful," and "Aren't we lucky to live
here?"

My heart is heavy, time has no meaning, your absence
overwhelms me
and I rush to the sanctuary of the home we planned
together for our special years.

Why did death separate us so unkindly darling?
Please, oh please, walk beside me again today - I miss you
so.

Claire Wright, Tewkesbury, Gloucestershire

*In remembrance of my husband, Reg, the love of my life, and
my inspiration.*

THE NATURE OF THINGS

Just for you
The good earth on its imaginary axis spins
And with its sluggish revolutions timely brings
Day and night to all creatures
In their turn.

Just for you
Before its fulminating majesty declines
The sun, incandescent in a cloudless blue sky, shines
Pure bright light upon all things
In their turn.

Just for you
The mottled moon with enigmatic purpose smiles
And with silvery light beams perfectly beguiles
The nocturnal forms of all things
In their turn.

And just for you
Amid the bottomless void of celestial space
Stellar diamonds twinkle and wink apace
At those below, working to explain how you fashioned
The nature of all things in their turn.

Bob Wilson, Corse Lawn, Gloucestershire

A HYMN TO SARAH

In such a restless age as ours, sharing
Walpole's Herries and wild Borrowdale, daring
to climb, from Castle Crag to Striding Edge
through legends born of Lake and Fell.
For this I praise thee.

Those memories I hold, close in my heart,
Of mountain, Fortress, Judith Paris and Vanessa.
And how they drew us, from the very start,
to lesser vales; then back to sterner rocks in Wales.
To these you took me.

Then on to Sprinkling Tarn whose icy dip took breath away
one exhilarating, gladly tiring day.
Or trapped on ice below the frozen awe-ful Scafell,
then high Crib Goch's stupendous razor edge and cliffs.
With these you thrilled me.

And now? Only dreams recall those wondrous hills,
revive the scents from Lakeland burning logs,
treasuring past thrills, and shepherd's fleeting dogs.
With Catbells dark towards the western sky and moonlit
sea,
With such hymns I sing praise to thee.

Brian D Lancaster, Mickleton, Gloucestershire

A YES THAT I COULD KISS

What do I say about you?
What images can I use to account for you?
You make me feel like a pastel,
You are an oil pastel and I am a chalk pastel
You conjure a lust. Something unsaid,
Sincere, rooted in the silence from which it grows.
A mmm, a yes that I could kiss.
You on me,
Your legs tucked in, the curve of you,
The words shoulder, lover and lap get stuck in my mind,
Your expressions line my head like wax.
It confuses me,
I wonder what it is that I'm feeling,
What it is that runs off my shoulders,
Down my arms and drips from my fingertips.
I will sleep in it.

Barney Sprague, Gloucester, Gloucestershire

ANNA

You can't contain yourself
Your bones are claustrophobic in your skin
He's set you off like a catherine wheel
Now none of it seems real
You're waiting for a spark to catch
To burn his hello's to goodbye's
It's so clear to you when he's there
When you're apart
You feel shadows passing through you,
One day you'll be so high
The fall will kill you
Without him you're sadness wins
You think you're the biggest loser of them all
Poor Anna in love

Angharad Williams, Trowbridge, Wiltshire

THE LONELY MAN

In the stillness silence shouting
Lonely is the lonely man,
Friendless, cheerless, days the same
Each reflecting yesterday
People passing smiling laughing
Each a life with happiness found
Darkness to come, a friend to enfold him
Till the cold light of day lays his lonely heart bare
Pity the lonely with nothing to cling to
Memories maybe but dim in the past
A past of remembering
A present of longing
A future of loneliness still yet to come

Jimima Shaw, Poole, Dorset

AN ALCOHOLIC IN HIS UNDERPANTS

An alcoholic in his underpants
advancing militantly on France
was impeded by the English Channel.

Staggering in non-alcoholic liquid,
he punched each puritanical wave,
shouting, "Bastard!"

Drained at last of hatred,
he retreated to his cider bottle,
flung his face at the sun
and exercised his adam's apple.

Collapsing on the shingle,
he slept immediately
with the subtle smile
of a dead man.

Peter Gillott, Mere, Wiltshire

AFTERWARDS

After he died, after the easy tears,
There was the silence, emptiness of grief,
And loneliness to kill the heart,
When he was gone, after so many years.

Where had he gone? How could so large a part
Of loving, caring, rage and joy
On a long instant vanish into air,
Leaving that grey and shrunken face
On a white pillow, in an empty room?

But it is Spring, and still the birds sing loud
Flowers and blossom riot into bloom,
The wind blows sweet across a greening world
That does not care.
This vast and splendid pageant still goes on.
After he's gone.

Lorna Harding, Salisbury, Wiltshire

ROSE

Rose
All I need is bravery,
Clarity and simplicity from you.
You're my rose.

We haven't even spoken.
You're my rose.

All that I can do is hope
Wait and watch your petals float,
From your bed late tonight
Smell you with the morning dew when you rise.
You're my rose.

Pick you from the bunch in front.
You're my rose.

See you bloom maybe on the occasional eve
It's not a surprise to me,
How beautiful you can be.
You're my rose.

Paul M Thomas, Swindon, Wiltshire

YOU

Your smile makes me happy
Like no one else's can,
It makes me realise that I'm so lucky
To have you as my man.

I've never had these feelings
That you make me get,
In fact I never knew what love was
Until we met.

When I hold you and kiss you
And you say you love me too,
I know that deep down inside
My heart belongs to you.

Natasha Stoakes, Trowbridge, Wiltshire

TO A SHY LOVER

My love,
Let's put away the masks,
And drop the proper phrases.

In this velvet dark,
Where touch falls soft as Cupid's wing,
Souls can speak without speech,
Hearts can heed without hearing.

Love is thoughtless of time,
But still time passes.

Therefore I say:
Waste not this night,
But let us haste to know each other.

Philippa Adburgham, Bristol, Avon

I WILL NOT WALK AWAY AGAIN

If I were a lesser friend, I'd say goodbye and walk away
But I will not walk away again from Loves behoving,
I will stand and be burned by Love, the fire of purification.
If I were a lesser friend I'd blame you, be arrogant, cold and
aloof,
I'd be distant and unconcerned for your pain.
I may begin with blame, but end with remorse
For my words, my silence and lack of love -
And in the end want to walk into that flame again
To find the Love that we are.
I walked away before, and in that loss
Ever walked away with a heavier heart.
I will not walk away again, as if I feel my feet are lead.
I will challenge you, challenge me, challenge us
To have the courage to love each other's pain;
Love enough to heal the other and so heal ourselves;
Love enough to know that the tear of the other
Is the tear of our own heart's eye.
No, or! I do not want to walk away, dear friend,
I do not want to walk away again.

Elana Freeman, Glastonbury, Somerset

HOW CAN I FORGET

A vision before me, I stare at your face,
I gently reach out, each line will I trace.
Memories stir as I look back in time,
Dearest father, you'll always be mine.

There to protect me, I came to no harm,
Always to guide me with wit and with charm.
To pick up the pieces when I was down.
The crease of your forehead when you would frown.

Life could be hard in many a way,
Teaching me values I still heed today.
Be truthful and honest, show that I care,
Close by my side you'll always be there.

Hearing the laughter, just as before,
Still there to guide me, the dad I adore.
I am afraid it wasn't to be,
Your time had come, you had to leave me.

Dearest father, how can I forget?
I'll remember you always, with love and respect.
Now I'm alone, I feel so bereft,
The vision before me is all I have left.

Joan Lake, Weston-Super-Mare, Somerset

WHITE MAN

Everything in life was painted,
So it looked beautiful and just right.
But what happened to the white man?
We are really mottled, what a sight!

I guess He ran out of colour,
And put all the oddments in a pot.
Trouble is they didn't mix together,
We are a mottled lot!

Pink brown, blue, mauve, yellow and white,
Clear part, so you can see through.
Really lucky, he had some oddments,
Or you'd see the works, what a to do!

Still, he had a great sense of humour,
That white man didn't understand.
Must have known they'd all be critics,
So watched as they defined their stand!

In winter we are all mauve and blotchy,
In summer we fight to get a tan.
So if people are really honest,
There is no such thing as a white man!

Ann Beard, Bridgwater, Somerset

MATERIAL GIRL

We have not met till now,
Two strangers in a bar, the smoke-haze at our feet.
A Gucci bag. A slim profile. A honeyed tongue. A painted
smile.
Time aches on. She's real. She's here.

We have not met till now,
Yet I've seen her in the shadows of my eyes,
Stalking the silence, she binds my tongue,
Basking in pregnant pauses.
She feasts, sleek and firm,
Upon the corpses of memory,
Upon words, ravaged by time.

We have not met till now,
Yet I've heard her silken murmur in my numbness,
Whispering words that blend and merge
To stroke the tender pulses of my failure.
She drips disdain from high-arched brows
To smoulder in the hollow shell of fairy-dust to ashes,
Ashes, to dust.

We have not met till now.
A cardboard cut-out propped against the substance of my
dreams.

Laura Butcher, Wiveliscombe, Somerset

THINKING OF YOU

Sitting in my room
watching the sun come up
jets weave their trails in the sky
sometimes I forget to swallow
sometimes I forget to breathe
thinking of you.

Sitting in my room
reading Henry Miller books
or surfing the world wide web
sometimes I forget to wonder
sometimes I forget to sleep
thinking of you.

Sitting in my room
smoking another cigarette
or drinking another beer
sometimes I forget to worry
sometimes I forget to dream
thinking of you.

Dave Stockley, Bristol, Avon

MOON GODDESS

As the sun sets in the west
where lies Avalon, Amenti, the Isle of the Blest,
darkening the roseate skies
to shadowy light that plays tricks with my eyes.

For twilight has a magical hue
as the stars twinkle and the sky deepens to indigo blue
opening a stargate to the otherworld,
for in the stillness and silence of night my spirit unfurls.

From the sea the Moon Goddess rises
bringing luminous, silvery skies,
reflecting Her silvery pathway over the sea,
a magical, mysterious place to be.

The Moon Goddess is the muse and inspiration flows
under Her wondrous silvery glow,
for moonlight, starlight and the great cosmic sea
alights my spark of creativity.

Jane Marshall, Glastonbury, Somerset

*Dedicated to the return of the Goddess, the feminine aspect
of the divine source, to restore balance and harmony in the
world and to the memory of my dear cat, Babe.*

LATE NIGHT, LEAVING THROUGH RAIN

You sweep the rain from your dress
Silk caress, cool temptress, like you were
Panther sleek, animal streak
Wanton cry, beautiful lie

You duck through the deepest night
Softest white, secret flight, like you were
Marie Antoinette, Fin de Siecle
Gliding by, innocent spy

You reach for a note in the air
Final care, musical prayer, like you were
Dance hall worn, corset drawn
Quiet try, glassy eye

You yield to the rope from above
Tangled dove, silent love, like you were
Phoenix flame, lifting away
Rising high, delicate sky

All in the beautiful lie
All in the innocent spy
All in the glassy eye
All in the delicate sky

Matt Bartlett, Bridgwater, Somerset

OPEN DOOR

Please come into my story
You know I want you there
Just enter my open door
My love
And flop in my easy chair.
Stretch out and rest yourself
My sweet
And feel my waves of care
Come sip some Irish coffee
From my favourite tandem cup
And tell me 'bout your day-to-day
Until you've had enough.
Then open up your heart to me
And loose your silken hair
Then move in close beside me
As close as you may dare
And we'll slither into oneness
And float upon the air.

John Morgan, Yeovil, Somerset

John Morgan said: "I have painted pictures and written
poetry since I was a teenager in the 1960's. For the last 15
years I have been able to pursue my passion for the cre-
ative life as a full-time professional artist/poet. I am mar-
ried to Jennifer, my soulmate, for whom *Open Door* was
written. We have a daughter named Lou. As well as being a
widely exhibited and purchased artist, I am also a pub-
lished poet with three collections of poems available. For
details telephone me on 01935 420781 or write to 16
Woodlands Terrace, Mill Lane, Yeovil, Somerset, BA20
1NY."

AWAKE

To slumber in your bed, and sleep all night without the
light.
To reach a state of total rest when all day you did your
best.
To rest in dreams of days gone by.

But in your dreams you cannot cry.
Of those you lost in days gone by.
Good or bad those dreams you dream will be sad.

So sleep and dream, work, and play
Be part of someone's dream one day.
Do your best and God will do the rest?

Gerald Whyte, Bristol, Avon

Gerald Whyte said: "I wrote this poem for my wife. Both
her parents, Lil and Ron, died, also her brother Ronnie.
The saddest thing is to lose people you love. What better
way, is there to honour them by remembering them in a
poem?"

WHILE YOU WERE SLEEPING

Last night I woke
While you were sleeping
I watched your face
Till dawnlight came creeping

The moonlight shone
Right through your bones
Bathed you in silver
For my eyes alone

It made shadows
Of your silken lashes
Touched your hair
With starlight flashes

I couldn't tear
My eyes away
I didn't want
To greet the day

Sleeping, unknowing
You didn't see
The deepest love
You stirred in me

Carolyn Fittall, Weston-super-Mare, Somerset

VALEDICTION

Yes, I shall forget you
When the world goes crashing into chaos,
And infinity is snuffed out like a candle.
And yet I think if some Titanic hand
Dissolved the myriad universes
I should be left behind to stand in the abyss of desolate
space,
My heart full of the love which once belonged to you.

And in the distance a figure is moving towards me slowly,
nearer,
And, yes, I rush, I rush to meet you
And close you in my arms.

A mirage;
They close on space
And I am left alone, alone to weep and love.

Beryl M Newport, Brislington, Bristol, Avon

Beryl M Newport said: "I was Educated at Colston's Girls'
School, Bristol and St Hilda's College, Oxford, I wrote quite
a lot of poetry in my late teens and early twenties.
Thereafter I became too busy with teaching, travelling,
being a married housewife and generally living. Now retired,
I find myself interested in writing poetry again."

I MISS YOU

I miss you in the morning
Also in the night
I miss you when it's dark
Also when it's light

When I have my breakfast
My dinner and my tea
I miss you at the table
You are all the world to me

But like the little fledgelings
That rest up in the tree
You had to fly from the nest
From my apron strings be free

There is an ache inside my heart
That no one else can see
It's the pain of loneliness
But of course it has to be

When your children fly the nest
And you're feeling free
You'll get that ache inside your heart
Just the same as me

Violetta J Ferguson, Burnham-on-Sea, Somerset

MOTHER

She is the diamond of my life,
Her brilliance shines on me.
She is my pole star;
Constantly guiding me.

She is my holy sun too.
Burning herself, yet giving
My energy and life too.

Like a sponge, she
Absorbs my pain.
By the osmosis of
Her selfless love; I
Have become turgid with,
Her true warmth of passion.

Symbolic and sweet nurturing,
Is the constant relationship
She is one sweet,
Sweetest in my life.
She is one precious possession,
I wish to own,
All my life.

Jyoti Kumar, Bristol, Avon

FOR RAY

Now that you are not here
There is a deep silence
In the house.
For when you were here
Your presence made music,
Felt by me but not recorded.
It sings in my memory
Now that you are not here.

Caroline Toll, Frome, Somerset

YOUR MEMORY

The scent of rose is your breath
The lilac hue your dew
The dew the tears in your eyes
As I turn and see those blue
Irises the streak of pain
Which now I'm passing through
Trampled bluebells hang their heads
Ashamed at what I do.

Your scent is lost on the breeze
Your presence distanced from my tread
Your tears and sobs
Threatening rain ahead
Knarled branches tear and scratch my face
Uneven stones my bare feet maim
Relief is what I feel right now
But later on the pain
That void called time alone cries out
Oh, what did I do?

Anna Arbaney, Bath, Somerset

THE LOSERS

I took the dog and went a walk,
I met a lady, stopped to talk.
She chattered long about her life,
Her man was ill, she was his wife.
He moaned and groaned about his lot,
She'd been ill too - that he forgot.
She did her best to soothe his pain
And if she failed, she tried again.
"Oh dear", she said, "I'll never win",
"Nor me", I gasped, "I married his twin."

Rita Humphreys, Bridgwater, Somerset

NEXT

Saturday night at the barbers
All was quiet and still
It had been closed for hours
No cash left in the till
As I peered through the window
I couldn't believe what I could see
And old black leather barber's chair
Was moving closer to me
then the glass door swung open
And a voice said "Come inside"
So I went on in to greet it
I was so sure it was alive
Just as I settled in the chair
And chose a style for my hair
It began to rise, high up into the air
I couldn't move for fear, I wouldn't dare
The cut throat razor closed in upon my neck.
Then I was woken by the barber
Shaking me and calling "next."

G M Wyatt, Weston-super-Mare, Somerset

SENTIMENTS FOR ISOLDE

Poetry should not be lugubrious and long
But short and strong.
Not tedious like Catholic devotions
But a précis of emotions.
Nor should it be stringent and terse
But of compact verse,
A lilting ode
In sing-song mode
That when read through
Simply states I love you.

John Leah, Winscombe, Somerset

MY WIFE, MY VALENTINE

Of all the girls I've ever known, and there have been a few;
Not one did captivate my heart, in the way you do.
With a smile just like the promise, of morning's early sun,
You light the spark inside me, then fill each day with fun
And when I say, those magic words, the all important
three.
Misty eyed, you kiss my lips, and snuggle close to me.
When I perceive this bleak old world, through the bottom of
a glass;
You lift me up, on gossamer wings, until the devils pass.
For a while, I am the man, I always used to be;
So from my heart, my very soul, I pledge these words to
thee;
My message on this Valentines Day, reflects our life
together;
I loved you then, I love you now, I'll love you dear forever.

John White, Chard, Somerset

*To my dear wife Dot, who has been my inspiration in all
things. The last line says it all.*

CHELTENHAM RAIN

The summer broken
We hurry umbrella-less
From town hall to theatre
Ducking raindrops,
Skirting puddles.

This eighteenth autumn
Brings to the old patter
A young woman's light footsteps
Moving to make a difference
Under tomorrow's new rain.

Sally Coniam, Bristol, Avon

CONGRATULATIONS

Oh romantic, foolish chap is he
Who plights his troth 'pon bended knee.
'twas half the way round the world
His undying love that he unfurled.

Heart a pounding, ruddy faced,
A ring upon her finger placed.
Popped the question, she said "Yes",
Then both got drunk. Oh! What a mess!

Drunk in love, the happy pair
To each other now did declare
To be together for time to come,
Sharing a love that's second to none.

It's grand to see romance lives on,
Treasure it well and you can't go wrong.
Of life's rich pleasures, it's one of the best,
So keep it exciting, love does the rest.

Brian H Clifford, Radstock, Somerset

PICTURE OF PEACE

Hands up high, sleeping.
A new born baby
All dressed in white.

Picture of peace
Having no worries.

Life is just beginning,
Let's hope life is kind
To her or him.
Who knows?

Georgina Martin, Yeovil, Somerset

TEACHER'S PET

You are my inspiration
You are this teacher's pet
If there is a brighter star
I haven't seen it yet.

You bring no restraints or barriers
To impede your rapid learning
But bring to every session
A heart that's always burning.

Every word that I enunciate
Transmits directly to your brain
Whatever tack I take
You always read the game.

I'll work for you forever
I'll forgo my usual fee
You remind me much of someone
You remind me much of me.

Trevor Carter, Bristol, Avon

189

YOU

You loved me, you hated me,
You calmed me, you frustrated me.
You hit me, you kicked me,
You cuddled me, you kissed me.
You listened, you spoke,
You angered, you provoked.
You matured, you grew,
You changed - but I knew
You'd always be the same to me
And I'll love you for eternity -
My child.

Pamela Bennie, Taunton, Somerset

PUPPY LOVE

I'll try not to bite you
Just post my master's letter
My doggy psychiatrist says
I'm now behaving better.

Come on Mr Postie
Please try and be brave
I will take the letter gently
I promise to behave.

I won't munch on your fingers
Or rip your clothes to shreds
Chase you across the garden
Leaping over flower beds.

I will not bite your bum
Or chase you down the street
In fact we could be chums
'Cause I'm really very sweet!

Kim Board, Ilminster, Somerset

LUCKY

She lived like a rebel.
At school, she said Eden's apple
Was the sweetest thing that fell.
She was Wendy in leather,
Flying Peter Pan style
To new adventures, dreamlike horizons.
Ready to take on
Anything, anyone.
She threw her penny
And every lucky pond
Kissed her blessing back.

Pamela Hill, Portishead, Avon

RENEWAL

You planted your beans on May the tenth
In the time-honoured country way.
Sowing the seed was an act of faith
That you would be there for the harvest
Come what may.

You repeated the ritual every spring:
Turning the oil and sieving it fine.
As you spaced out the dark purple kidneys so
You placed a stake in the future
In sticks and twine.

With the late spring rain came the first limp tendrils,
Runners ablaze as plants unfold.
But where are you now? You are no more.
Your life has ended; your garden untended.
What remains is decay
And vegetable mould.

Margaret Andow, Bristol, Avon

GRACEFUL OLD LADIES

Graceful old ladies
With large cluster rings,
Commanding respect in each other.

Traditions so gay
With time-honoured skin,
Their heart-felt meaning of mother.

They build their walls
On aversion to change
And house themselves
With one another.

James Haxworth, Bristol, Avon

YOU

I hear music when I look at you.
A beautiful theme of every dream I ever knew.
Down deep in my heart I hear it played,
I feel it start then melt away.
I hear music when I touch your hand,
A beautiful melody from some enchanted land.
Deep down in my heart I hear it say,
"Is this the day?"

I alone have heard this lovely strain.
I alone have heard this glad refrain.
Must it be, forever inside of me?
Why can't I let it go, why can't I let you know?
Why can't I let you know the song
My heart would sing?
That beautiful rhapsody of love and young and spring
The music is sweet, the words are true,
The song is you.

John Windsor, Bridgwater, Somerset